The Royal Court Theatre presents

Jonathan

Harvey's

BABIES

First performed at the Royal Court Theatre on
5th September 1994

Originally developed and presented at the Royal
National Theatre Studio

The Royal Court Theatre is financially assisted by the Royal
Borough of Kensington and Chelsea.

Recipient of a grant from the Theatre Restoration Fund &
from the Foundation for Sport & the Arts

The Royal Court's Play Development Programme
is funded by the Audrey Skirball-Kenis Theatre

Registered Charity number 231242

HOW THE ROYAL COURT IS BROUGHT TO YOU...

The English Stage Company at the Royal Court Theatre is supported financially by a wide range of public bodies and private companies, as well as its own trading activities. The theatre receives its principal funding from the **Arts Council of Great Britain**, which has supported the Royal Court since 1956. The **Royal Borough of Kensington & Chelsea** gives an annual grant to the Royal Court Young People's Theatre and provides some of its staff. The **London Boroughs Grants Committee** contributes to the cost of productions in the Theatre Upstairs.

Other parts of the Royal Court's activities are made possible by business sponsorships. Several of these sponsors have made a long term commitment. 1994 saw the fourth Barclays New Stages Festival of Independent Theatre, which has been supported throughout by **Barclays Bank**. **British Gas North Thames** has so far supported three years of the Royal Court's Education Programme. Now in its 26th year, the Young Writers' Festival has been sponsored by **Marks & Spencer** since 1991. The latest sponsorship by **WH Smith** has been to help make the launch of the new Friends of the Royal Court scheme so successful.

We are particularly grateful to the **Audrey Skirball - Kenis Theatre** of Los Angeles for providing funding to support a series of work new to the Main Stage, the first of which is Jonathan Harvey's **BABIES**. 1993 saw the start of our association with the Audrey Skirball-Kenis Theatre. The Skirball Foundation is funding a Playwrights Programme at the Royal Court. Exchange visits for writers between Britain and the USA complement the greatly increased programme of readings and workshops which have fortified the Royal Court's capability to develop new plays.

The much expanded season of plays in the Theatre Upstairs by young new writers would not have been possible without the generous sponsorship of the **Jerwood Foundation**. The season is being produced in association with the **Royal National Theatre Studio**.

In 1988 the Royal Court launched the **Olivier Building Appeal** to raise funds to restore, repair and improve the theatre building. So far nearly £700,000 has been raised. The theatre has new bars and front of house areas, new roofs, air conditioning and central heating boilers, a rehearsal room and a completely restored and cleaned facade. This would not have been possible without a very large number of generous supporters and significant contributions from the **Theatres' Restoration Fund**, the **Rayne Foundation**, the **Foundation for Sport and the Arts** and the **Arts Council's Incentive Funding Scheme**.

The **Gerald Chapman Award** was founded in 1988 to train and develop young theatre directors. It is now jointly funded by the Royal Court and **BBC Television**. The **ITV Companies** fund the **Regional Theatre Young Directors Scheme**, with which the Royal Court has been associated for many years.

The Royal Court earns the rest of money it needs to operate from the Box Office, from other trading and from the transfers of plays such as **Death and the Maiden**, **Six Degrees of Separation** and **Oleanna** to the West End. But without public subsidy it would close immediately and its unique place in British Theatre would be lost. The Arts Council has had its grant from the government cut by £3.9 million for this year. This means large cuts and reductions in the amount of subsidised theatre activity. If you care about the future of arts in this country, please write to your MP and say so.

THE ROYAL NATIONAL THEATRE STUDIO

The Royal National Theatre Studio is complex of workspaces in the Old Vic Annexe, leased rent-free to the National by the owner of the Old Vic, Ed Mirvish.

As part of the over-all programme there are regular showings of work in progress to invited audiences. But the Studio doesn't give public performances. Freedom from pressure is central to the way of working. At the same time, the Studio is a theatrical set-up not an academic one. It's exhilarating to present your work in private, but you do from time to time wonder what the public might think of it. This is why Studio work has regularly emerged at other addresses: in small-scale London theatres or on the South Bank - at the Queen Elizabeth Hall or at the National itself.

Trips abroad are part of the game: **TRACKERS OF OXYRHYNCHUS** in Greece, a 1992 learning and teaching expedition to Lithuania, or (in Autumn 1994) a historic visit to post-apartheid South Africa. **"Springboards"** (in 1993) was a major emergence: a celebration of new drama - not only written, but devised, improvised, even sung - which linked the Cottesloe Theatre, the Bush, the Theatre Upstairs and four regional theatres.

BABIES is different again. The focus this time is exclusively on the text-based play: an endangered species these days, given the time and money it takes to put on a play in a first-class manner, let alone the bizarre myths which accumulate around new writing - that audiences don't like it, for example, or that it peaked in 1956.

By joining forces with the Royal Court, we're able to capitalise on a shared commitment to nurturing and encouraging new writing. And - as became clear while swapping scripts and pooling opinions - a shared delight in the daring and vivacity of the new playwrights of today.

BABIES

Jonathan Harvey

The Royal Court Writers Series published by
Methuen Drama in association with the Royal Court Theatre

Methuen Drama Royal Court Writers Series

Babies was first published in Great Britain
in the Royal Court Writers Series in 1994
by Methuen Drama
in association with the Royal Court Theatre,
Sloane Square, London SW1N 8AS

ISBN 0-413-69220-5

A CIP catalogue record for this book
is available from the British Library

Typset by Wilmaset, Birkenhead, Wirral

Coming next...

The Royal Court's Autumn Season is being presented in association with the Royal National Theatre Studio, with sponsorship from the Jerwood Foundation and the Audrey Skirball-Kenis Theatre.

Main House

From 27th October
THE EDITING PROCESS
by Meredith Oakes
directed by Stephen Daldry

From 6th December
The Royal Court and Out of Joint present
THE LIBERTINE
by Stephen Jeffreys
in repertoire with
THE MAN OF MODE
by George Etherege

Theatre Upstairs

From 13th October
COMING ON STRONG
The Royal Court/Marks & Spencer Young Writers' Festival

From 10th November
PEACHES
by Nick Grosso
directed by James Macdonald

From 1 December
ASHES AND SAND
by Judy Upton
directed by Ian Rickson

BABY TALK.

Jonathan Harvey talks to Robin Hooper, the Royal Court's Literary Manager.

RH: When you first came into the room, Jonathan, you took off your bomber jacket and put it on the back of your bum like an Edwardian bustle. Why do you do that sort of thing?

JH: Because you were on the phone and I wanted to get your attention. So I did a bit of flamenco dancing for you. And it worked. I became instantly more interesting than the other person on the end of the phone and you said, "Listen I have to go."

RH: It seems you don't have any difficulty at all coming into a space.

JH: Oh I do. I know you. And I feel comfortable with you.

RH: So that means you're a bit shy?

JH: I wouldn't do that with everybody. I mean I'm not a luvvie. I love all the luvviness of the business. But there's still a part of me which thinks I'm not putting up with that and oh I've got to meet them have I ? There's still a part of me which is still quite Liverpudlian.

RH: I had some experience of working in Liverpool in the early seventies. There was a very exciting theatre there at the time called the Everyman. Willy Russell was starting to write his plays. It seemed to me that a city like that would cough up a wonderful culture. And I'm not just talking about the theatre. There was poetry and music. Do you think it's still like that twenty years on? Does it still have that kind of specialness?

JH: No. Because if that was the case then I'd be having my stuff put on in Liverpool and hopefully it would transfer to London. I think I would be living in Liverpool now. I was very lucky to grow up there because in the eighties the media was just full of Liverpool, so you didn't question the fact that you can come from Liverpool and be a writer. For instance, there were things like "Boys from the Black Stuff" and "Educating Rita" and "Letter to Brezhnev". And it was all sort of seeing places and people you knew. And your own life echoed on the screen or in the theatre. It was exciting and encouraging. And I don't know whether I would have got that living elsewhere.

RH: Do you really think it has suffered as a city and as a community? Not just on a cultural level but on every kind of level.

JH: It has suffered. I was ten when Thatcher got in. I'm aware that it has declined, because of stories and the way my parents look at the city now. It's like a feeling it's had its day, which is an unpopular thought to have about Liverpool, being from Liverpool, because there is a very fierce loyalty to it. That's part of the reason why I don't write plays set there. You're always very aware of showing the good side of Liverpool and that's not a good thing to have when writing something because you want it to be honest. That's why I set things in London. I want Liverpool to be this marvellous city that you remember. But going back I find it quite a hard city and macho.

RH: As a gay young man in Liverpool did you have some difficulty ? Were you aware that you were different as a teenager ?

JH: I was aware from primary school age. I remember my nan went to a parents' evening at school and they said " Well, Jonathan plays with the girls a lot " And she came home and said "You can't do that or you'll get called a cissy " And I said "Well I'm always called a cissy ". Having said that I don't think it would be different wherever I grew up because that male image is everywhere. But my dad, you see, isn't your typical macho Liverpool father. We are very similar. I feel quite lucky.

RH: When did you actually come to live in London ?

JH: Well, I lasted four years in Hull doing a degree part of which was to train as a teacher. I then applied for twelve jobs in London as a teacher.

RH: And at the same time there was this beginning of an interest in your work as a playwright ?

JH: My first play was on at the Liverpool Playhouse when I was eighteen. It was called "The Cherry Blossom Tree". While I was at university I wrote another called "Mohair" which I sent to the Royal Court's Young Writer's Festival here, and it was produced. So I had a few plays done. I would have loved to have jacked everything in to be a writer but I didn't. I looked for teaching jobs thinking I'll do it for one year, or however long I need to do it before you can be a supply teacher. Then I can go three days a week, do supply, and write for two days a week. But I got a job. I never thought I'd be any good as a teacher. I thought I'd hate it. And I ended up loving it.

RH: How did you get on as a school boy ?

JH: I went to the "Blue Coat School". It was very strict and disciplinarian and tried very hard to be like a private school. I didn't want to go to school one day because I'd lost my hymn book. And I knew the wrath of the gods would fall on me by Mr Pinder, the music teacher. He used to sit there and play "The Archers" theme music on the piano as we walked into music lesson. He loved me actually because I was a choir boy.

RH: I thought you were going to say something else there.

JH: He used to have suspenders on his socks. Weird. Everyone was petrified of losing their hymn book. So when I was a teacher I then had to reassess what I thought was right and wrong. I had my own tutor group. I wasn't really bothered if they lost the equivalent of a hymn book. Little things I think I got right to help the bigger things get better. If they left their pencil case at home then I would have spare ones in my desk to give to them to use that day.

RH: So basically you were a human being ?

JH: I was to start with but by the end, you see, the thing I don't like about teaching is that it turns you into a bit of a fascist. I remember there was this girl in my class who kept on coming in with make up on. You'd go "You've got lipstick on "…. "No I haven't" So I'd ring her mother up. And she would say "Well you see, Mr Harvey. she puts it on before she goes to sleep. So when she wakes up in the morning her lips are dyed by it so that when she says that to you she ain't got lipstick on, she's telling the truth." "I don't care. Get it off."

RH: Still I don't detect with you any real frustration or unhappiness about being a teacher which to a certain extent is rare.

JH: It is rare.

RH: From what I know about you and your work there seems to be an inherent sense of what is right and what is wrong in your personality. Was there any confusion about this sense of morality if you like,in being a young gay man?

JH: I never felt it was wrong.

RH: A lot of gay men do though don't they?

JH: Yes…. I don't really understand… I remember thinking well maybe I should feel it's wrong because I had a very strict church upbringing as well.

RH: What was that?

JH: Church of England. I was expected to go to church every week and I went until the age of eighteen. Society was telling me it was wrong, but I didn't see what was wrong because it was just inside me and it was natural. But there was guilt thinking "Oh what's my Mum and Dad going to think?"

RH: A good deal of the best playwriting concerns itself with a sense of morality in the world. We're being forced to address this issue particularly at present. For instance the whole exposure of child abuse, with "kids who kill" and the consequent obsession in the media. What do you think has gone wrong? Generally speaking, what is being said, is that it's lack of parental care and control.

JH: I'm afraid I agree with them. There's a lot to be said for parental responsibility. Having said that actually, in BABIES I'm celebrating the marvellous parents. I think that mother in the play is a terrific woman. I wanted her to be very special, very unconventional. And as for the kids themselves, I was lucky enough to leave them when they were fourteen. I made them older in the play and just about to hit that vile bit of puberty. I had them young and they were little babies.

RH: Just to return to the theatre for a second, you insist that you're not a luvvie?

JH: I'm not a luvvie in the way I haven't been to Oxford. My parents were never in the business. I've read one Shakespeare play. I don't really know much. I'm a bit thick sometimes. But I do love all the business. When I was a kid my Mum got me a membership of the Liverpool Record Library. I used to come home every week with "My Fair Lady" "West Side Story"...
I used to do interviews with myself. My Dad had a tape recorder and I used to interview myself as Charmian Carr who played Leisl in "The Sound of Music". My Mum said "It's not normal a boy your age to be into musicals." I wanted to be a nun. I wanted to be Julie Andrews. I wanted all that. And denied myself it I suppose in my teenage years. I mean I love telly. I've grown up with television.

RH: Does your love for it then have something to do with energy or getting your own back through the media of television or theatre?

JH: Possibly. Because sometimes I think the rough lads at my school say "Oh Harvey's a queer" or "Harvey's a snob" , because I had a more feminine Liverpool accent than them, I think oh well it'll be interesting to see if they've read that piece on me in the Guardian. I bumped into one of them in Liverpool once and he said "Oh God you're a bit of a star now aren't you?" There is that side to it. I think also my family are great television lovers. It's marvellous for me to be able to ring up my Mum and Dad and say I met whoever from your favourite television programme last night. There is that obsession with fame.

RH: And music itself obviously...

JH: I've just bought a video recorder and much to the embarrassment of my friends, the first videos I bought were "Mary Poppins", "Chitty Chitty Bang Bang", "Carousel" (I wept through that last night) and my friends are all saying why didn't I get "Eraserhead" or "The Crying Game" ?

RH: Do you like the popular stuff ? Who do you like ?

JH: I love "Take That". I like any music really. I'm a musical whore I think. I like using music to help me with the writing where it can express something you can't say, or ironically add humour.

RH: Do you think you could write a libretto ?

JH: I don't really because I think it's a bit of an outdated form now. Songs mean different things now. I can never understand family and friends when they say "O God!!" when you watch a musical on screen and suddenly somebody bursts out singing. I love that bit most. When people express themselves. I've been listening to Doris Day quite a lot lately. I just think the opening to "Pillow Talk" would be a lovely way to open a show. With the lights going down...."Doo diddi doo diddi doo.....Pillow Talk.....doo di doo.....Bum chichi bum....." What a marvellous way to open a play about people looking for love. It inspires me. So use it !

RH: I think that'll do Jonathan.

BABIES

by Jonathan Harvey

CAST *in alphabetical order*

Vivian Williams	**Lorraine Ashbourne**
Ivy Williams / Valerie Pinkney	**Helen Blatch**
Drag Queen	**Reginald S. Bundy**
Gemma Sweeney	**Joann Condon**
Woody / Kenny	**Karl Draper**
Kelly	**Sharon Duncan Brewster**
Joe Casey	**Ian Dunn**
Sonia Sweeney	**Elizabeth Estensen**
David	**Ricci Harnett**
Manda	**Louise Heaney**
Ernie Sweeney	**Kenneth MacDonald**
Richard	**Simon Sherlock**
Tammy	**Melissa Wilson**
Tammy's Friends	**Kerry Bradshaw, Caroline Carmody, Emily Jo Chaney, Elisha Holligan, Stevie Houston, Korhan Hussain, Michelle Ianiello, Lucie Johnston, Waheed Mohammed, Natasha Gill, Anyia Nwaka, Jacqui Thomas, Aisling O'Neil Zambon.**

Director	**Polly Teale**
Designer	**Bunny Christie**
Lighting Designer	**Johanna Town**
Sound	**Paul Arditti**
Stage Manager	**Caroline Hawes**
DSM	**Kevin Fitzmaurice**
ASM	**Hedda Moore**
Student ASM	**Natasha Roffe**
Assistant Director	**Jeremy Herrin**
Fight Director	**Terry King**
Voice Coach	**Jeanette Nelson**
Costume Supervisor	**Jennifer Cook**
Production Photographer	**Ivan Kyncl**

The performance lasts approximately 2 hours and 40 minutes. There will be an interval of 15 minutes

BABIES BIOGRAPHIES

JONATHAN HARVEY (author)

For the Royal Court: Mohair (1988); Wildfire (1992). Other plays include: Rupert Street Lonely Hearts Club (1994 for the RNT Studio); Beautiful Thing (1993, Bush Theatre; 1994, Donmar Warehouse); Lady Snogs the Blues (1991, Lincoln Arts Festival); Catch (1990, Spring Street Studio, Hull); Tripping and Falling (1989, Glasshouse Theatre Co, Manchester); Cherry Blossom Tree (1987, Liverpool Playhouse Studio).

TV includes: Currently writing screenplay of Beautiful Thing for Tony Garnett at Island World; Teachers (also in development with Tony Garnett); Love Junkie (just finished screenplay for BBC TV); West End Girls (Carlton TV).

Mohair published by Hodder & Stoughton in First Lines.

United Kingdom representative at Interplay '88, the international Festival of Young Playwrights, Sydney, Australia, 1988.

Awards: George Devine Award 1993 (joint winner for BABIES); John Whiting Award 1994 for Beautiful Thing.

PAUL ARDITTI (Sound)

For the Royal Court: Thyestes, My Night With Reg, The Kitchen, The Madness of Esme and Shaz, Hammett's Apprentice, Hysteria, Live like Pigs, Search and Destroy.

Other theatre sound design includes: Hamlet (Peter Hall Company); St. Joan (Strand Theatre); The Winter's Tale, Cymbeline, The Tempest, Antony & Cleopatra, The Trackers of Oxyrhynchus (Royal National Theatre); The Gift of the Gorgon (RSC & Wyndham's); Orpheus Descending (Theatre Royal, Haymarket & Broadway); A Streetcar Named Desire (Bristol Old Vic); The Winter's Tale (Manchester Royal Exchange); The Wild Duck (Phoenix); Henry IV, The Ride Down Mount Morgan (Wyndams's); Born Again (Chichester Festival); Three Sisters, Matador (Queens); Twelfth Night, The Rose Tattoo (Playhouse); Two Gentlemen of Verona, Becket, Cyrano de Bergerac (Theatre Royal, Haymarket); Travesties (Savoy); Four Baboons Adoring the Sun (Lincoln Centre, 1992 Drama Desk Award); Piaf (Piccadilly).

Opera includes: Gawain (ROH).

TV includes: The Camomile Lawn.

LORRAINE ASHBOURNE

For the Royal Court: The Kitchen, Land of the Living. Other theatre includes: The Brothers Karamazov, The Odd Women, She Stoops to Conquer (Best Actress, Manchester Evening News); She's in Your Hands, Your Home in the West, Dr. Heart (Manchester Royal Exchange); Three Girls in Blue (West Yorkshire Playhouse); An Italian Straw Hat (Shaftesbury Theatre); Jane Eyre (Birmingham Rep); Canterbury Tales (Leicester Haymarket); All My Sons, Blood Brothers (York Theatre Royal); The Genius (Newcastle Playhouse); See How They Run (Theatr Clwyd); It Runs in the Family, Steaming, When I Was a Girl I Used to Scream & Shout (Westcliff Palace).

TV includes: Chillers No. 6, Casualty, In Suspicious Circumstances, 3,7,11; The Bill, Fighting for Gemma, Mr. Wroe's Virgins, London's Burning, Casualty, Bread, Boon, Rich Tea & Sympathy.

Films include: Jack and Sarah, Distant Voices - Still Lives, The Dressmaker, Resurrected.

Radio includes: Red Devils.

HELEN BLATCH

For the Royal Court: Live Like Pigs.

Theatre includes: Long Day's Journey into Night, Ghosts, Hamlet, King Lear, The Importance of Being Earnest, Abingdon Square (Soho Poly); The Gift of the Gorgon (RSC & Wyndham's); Pericles, All's Well that Ends Well, Columbus and the Discovery of Japan (RSC); Julius Caesar, Sex Please We're Italian, The Snow Queen (Young Vic).

TV includes: A Touch of Frost, The Bill, The Buddha of Suburbia, Coronation Street, London Embassy, The Practice, A Doll's House, Doctor Who, The Secret Army, Peer Gynt, Katherine Mansfield.

Films include: A Doll's House.

REGINALD S. BUNDY

For the Royal Court: Night After Night (also on tour in the US & UK).

Other theatre includes: Fiddler on the Roof (original West End production); Elegies for Punks & Raging Queens (Criterion); A Vision of Love Revealed in Sleep (Gloria at the Drill Hall); seasons at London Palladium, Queens Theatre, Westcliff Palace, Yvonne Arnaud Theatre, Roundhouse.

Cabaret includes: The Disappointer Sisters, Regina Fong - Last of the Romanoffs, Bloolips.

TV includes: Co-hosted Channel Four's Club X; Now That It's Morning (Channel Four).

Films include: Oh! What a Lovely War!; The Slipper and the Rose.

BUNNY CHRISTIE (Designer)

For the Royal Court: The Terrible Voice of Satan, Hammett's Apprentice.

Other theatre designs include: Chopped Hamlet, Carmen (Chichester); The Happy End (RSC); The Changeling, The Mother (Manchester Contact Theatre); Lucy's Play, Kathie & The Hippopotamus (Edinburgh Traverse); A Matter of Life and Death, The Mother, Yerma (with Pamela Howard); Twelfth Night, Roots, The Long Way Round, At Our Table, Billy Liar (RNT); Electra and Orestes, All's Well that Ends Well (Leicester Haymarket); The Hypochondriac (Leicester Haymarket & Lyric, Hammersmith); Mary Rose (Greenwich); Pentecost, Coriolanus (Renaissance); Married Love (Wyndham's); Hamlet (Bristol Old Vic); The Way to go Home, Once a Catholic, A Love Song for Ulster (Tricycle); The Price (Oxford Stage Co); The Dream, Hamlet, A Doll's House, As You Like It (Century); The Mill on the Floss (Shared Experience); The Playboy of the Western World (Birmingham Rep).

Opera designs include: The Marriage of Figaro, Lucia di Lammermoor, Cosi fan tutte (Opera 80), The Merry Widow (Scottish Opera).

Film & TV includes: Ill Fares the Land, The Prisoner, Swansong.

JOANN CONDON
Theatre includes: What's Wrong With Angry? (BAC); Drama (Greenwich Studio); The Restless Rug (TIE tour); Sell Out! (Etcetera); Midsummer Night's Dream, Hamlet (Burton-Taylor, Oxford); Humpty Dumpty (Panto tour); Last Laugh (Edinburgh Festival); New Age, The Great Audition, Foam (Half Moon).

KARL DRAPER
Theatre includes: Somewhere (RNT); Coyote Ugly (Old Red Lion); The Hatchet Man (DOC); The Millionairess (The Rose, Fulham); Arki-Types (Etcetera); Song of Myself (Greenwich).
TV includes: Oliver's Travels, Grushko, The Bill.

SHARON DUNCAN BREWSTER
TV includes: To Have and to Hold, King of Hearts, Video Dramas, Between the Lines, EastEnders, Grange Hill, 2.4 Children, Up the Garden Path, Starting Out.
Films include: Strong Kids Safe Kids.
Radio includes: Friends, Turn on the Tap, Something to Think About, The Lost Squearable, What the Others Say.

IAN DUNN
For the Royal Court: Six Degrees of Separation (& Comedy).
Other theatre includes: Somewhere (Liverpool, RNT); A Prayer for Wings (tour); Hidden Laughter (Vaudeville); Forget-Me-Not-Lane (Greenwich); Invisible Friends, Wolf at the Door, Brighton Beach Memoirs (Scarborough).
TV includes: Jackanory Gulf, The Merrihill Millionaires, The Bill, A Touch of Frost, Soldier Soldier, Children of the North.
Films include: American Friends, Bye Bye Baby.

ELIZABETH ESTENSEN
For the Royal Court: The Gorky Brigade.
Other theatre includes: John Paul George Ringo & Bert (Liverpool Everyman); Lenz (Hampstead); A Flea in her Ear, The Importance of Being Earnest, Bedroom Farce (Nottingham Playhouse); The Cherry Orchard (Riverside); Clouds (Criterion); Say Your Prayers (Joint Stock tour); A Midsummer Night's Dream (Open Air Theatre, Regents Park); Serjeant Musgrave's Dance, Don Juan (RNT); The Servant of Two Masters (Cambridge Arts & tour); La Ronde (Bristol Theatre Royal); Wait Until Dark (Nuffield Southampton & tour); Cavalcade (Chichester); The Play's the Thing (Cambridge Arts & Singapore Arts Festival); Hedda Gabler (Yvonne Arnaud, Guildford); Midsummer Night's Dream (Actors Company); Shirley Valentine (Duke of York's); Water Music (Soho Theatre Co); Richard III, Merry Wives of Windsor (Northern Broadsides at Riverside Studios).
TV includes: The Liver Birds, Elizabeth Alone, Our Day Out, The Ladies, Marmalade at Work, T Bag, Happy Families, Life Without George, Casualty, The Bill, The Upper Hand, A Touch of Frost: Appropriate Adults.

RICCI HARNETT
Theatre includes: The Criminal Prosecution of Animals (Luric Studio, Hammersmith).
TV includes: Men of the Month, A Better Life than Mine, The Bill, Teenage Health Freak, Pigboy, Grey Areas, Between the Lines.
Films include: Object of Beauty, The Old Curiosity Shop, Jack the Ripper.

LOUISE HEANEY
For the Royal Court: Wildfire (Theatre Upstairs & local tour).
TV & film includes: Sherlock Holmes, Safe, The Bill.

KENNETH MACDONALD
For the Royal Court: My Night With Reg.
Other theatre includes: It Ain't Half Hot Mum (Scarborough & Bournemouth); A Midsummer Night's Dream (Bedford Theatre Co); The Day War Broke Out (Sheffield Crucible & Bush); Macbeth (Shaw); The Second Mrs. Tanqueray, Jack & the Beanstalk (Lyceum, Crewe); Say Goodnight to Grandma (Belgrade); A Day in the Death of Joe Egg, Hadrian VII, A Touch of Purple (Leatherhead); Animal Farm (Royal National Theatre); The Cheeky Chappie (regional tour); Ladybird (Hyman & Kass tour); Private Times (Library Theatre).
TV includes: Only Fools & Horses, It Ain't Half Hot Mum, Last of the Summer Wine, Dad's Army, Come Back Mrs. Noah, The Dick Emery Show, The Cilla Black Show, Softly Softly, Z Cars, Tenko, One by One, Games Without Frontiers, Silas Marner, Chance of a Lifetime, Keep an Eye on Albert, Farmers Arms, Crimewatch, Brush Strokes, The Chain, The Famous Five, Upstairs Downstairs, Shine on Harvey Moon, Surgical Spirit, Brookside, Capital Lives.
Films include: Mixed Doubles, The Class of Miss McMichael, Hitch in Time, Breaking Glass, Singleton's Pluck.

SIMON SHERLOCK
Theatre includes: The Caretaker (Cockpit); Out of the Frying Pan, The Dying Game (London Schools tour); LoveBites, The Dying Game, Jumpshot (Riverside); The Man of Mode (BAC); Dr. Faustus (Edinburgh Festival); Polo (Lyric, Hammersmith).
TV includes: Safe.
Films include: Brotherly Love, Juvenile.
Miscellaneous: U2 Zooropa Tour, Wembley Stadium.

POLLY TEALE (Director)
Theatre includes: Mill on the Floss (Shared Experience at the Tricycle, co-Director Nancy Meckler); A Taste of Honey (English Touring Company); Somewhere (Cottesloe/Liverpool Playhouse); Waiting at the Water's Edge (Bush); Uganda, Manpower, The Stairwell, Flying, Other Voices Other Rooms (Royal National Theatre Studio); What Is Seized (Drill Hall); Ladies in the Lift (Soho Poly & tour); Now You See Me (Young Vic).
TV includes: A Better Life Than Mine, Afters (own screenplay shown on BBC2 Screen Two Series).
As a writer: Fallen (1987, Traverse Theatre, Drill Hall, Liverpool Playhouse: published by Women's Press).

1993/1994 Associate Director of Shared Experience
Theatre Co.
1984: winner of The Sunday Times Playwriting Award
at the National Student Drama Festival.

JOHANNA TOWN (Lighting Designer)
For the Royal Court: Road (1994), The Kitchen,
Hammett's Apprentice, The Terrible Voice of Satan,
Search and Destroy, Women Laughing, Faith Healer,
A Jamaican Airman Foresees his Death.
Other theatre lighting designs include: The Lodger
(Royal Exchange & Hampstead); Richard II (Royal
Exchange); Snow Orchid (London Gay Theatre); The
Set-Up, Crackwalker (Gate Theatre); Josephine
(BAC); Celestina (ATC); Beautiful Thing (Bush &
Donmar Warehouse); over 20 designs for Liverpool
Playhouse including Macbeth, The Beaux Stratagem,
Madame Mao.
Opera includes: The Marriage of Figaro, Eugene
Onegin, The Abduction from the Seraglio (Opera 80);
Human Voice, Perfect Swine (MTM); La Traviata
(MTL at the Donmar & in Hamburg).
Currently Chief Electrician at the Royal Court.

MELISSA WILSON
Theatre includes: The Owl and the Pussycat (?);
Boys Mean Business (Bush).
TV includes: Touch of Frost, The Bill, Poirot, The
Alleyn Mysteries, Casualty, Summer's Lease, 101
Things to do with Wood, The Diary of Rita Patel,
Polaski, London's Burning, Strike it Rich, Dance for
Ethiopia, No Adults Allowed, Walrus, Nanny, A
Midsummer Night's Dream, Union, Some of Our Best
Friends, The Gentle Touch, The Latchkey Children,
Kipling at Palemans, Tropic of Ruislip.
Films include: Memoirs of a Survivor, Enter the
Adventure, Supper at Emmaeus, Crush, The Friday
Fashion Show.
Radio includes: Up the Garden Path, The Orange
Story Tape.

TAMMY'S FRIENDS
are all Students at Kingsway College.
**KERRY BRADSHAW, CAROLINE CARMODY,
EMILY JO CHANEY, ELISHA HOLLIGAN, STEVIE
HOUSTON, KORHAN HUSSEIN, MICHELLE
IANIELLO, LUCIE JOHNSTON, WAHEED
MOHAMMED, NATASHA GILL, ANYIA NWAKA,
JACQUI THOMAS, AISLING O'NEILL ZAMBON.**

We would like to thank the following for their help with this
production: BBC Radio Leicester; The Manchester Tabacco
Company; The National Canine Defence League; Kwik Silver
Theatre Company; DHSS Newcastle Upon Tyne, Norcross,
Leeds; Toshiba; Sainsburys plc; Louis Vuitton; The Sporting
Life Ltd; Timex Corporation, UK Time Ltd; World Wide Fund
for Nature; Maclaren; W.A.Ingrams (Zippo) Ltd; Ruddles
Beer; Augustus Barnett; Sarah Beecham .
Wardrobe care by Persil and Comfort courtesy of Lever
Brothers Ltd; watches by The Timex Corporation; refrigerators
by Electrolux and Philips Major Appliances Ltd.; kettles for
rehearsals by Morphy Richards; video for casting purposes
by Hitachi; backstage coffee machine by West 9; furniture by
Knoll International; freezer for backstage use supplied by
Zanussi Ltd 'Now that's a good idea.' Hair by Carole at
Edmond's, 19 Beauchamp Place, SW3. Closed circuit TV
cameras and monitors by Mitsubishi UK Ltd. Natural spring
water from Wye Spring Water, 149 Sloane Street, London
SW1, tel. 071-730 6977. Overhead projector from W.H. Smith.

PATRONS
Christopher Bland
Diana Bliss
Henny Gestetner OBE
Gwen Humble
Ian McShane
John Mortimer
Richard Pulford
Richard Wilson
Irene Worth

CORPORATE PATRONS
Advanpress
Alan Baxter and Associates
Associated Newspapers Ltd
BMI Healthcare
Caradon plc
Carlton Communications
Compass Group plc
Criterion Productions plc
CS First Boston Ltd
Freshfields
Gardner Merchant Ltd

Homevale Ltd
Laporte plc
Lazard Brothers and Co Ltd
Lex Services PLC
New Penny Productions Ltd
Penguin Books Ltd
The Simkins Partnership
Simons Muirhead and Burton
Tomkings plc
Vodafone Group

ASSOCIATES
Robert Dufton
Robyn Durie
Nicholas A Fraser
Kingsmead Charitable Trust
Patricia Marmont
Peter Jones

BENEFACTORS
James R Beery
Mrs Denise Bouche
Carole Conrad
Conway Van Gelder
David Coppard & Co
Coppings Trust
Curtis Brown Ltd
Allan Davis
D M M Dutton
D T Dutton
Rocky Gottlieb
Granada Television Ltd
Romaine Hart
Andre Hoffman
Jarvis Hotels Ltd
Peter Job
Lady Lever
Ian Martin
Pat Morton
T J Norris
Michael Orr
Eric Parker
Pearson plc
Paola Piglia
Angharad Rees
Rentokil Group plc
Sears plc
Allan Sheppard
Swiss Bank Corporation
William Morris Agency

THE ENGLISH STAGE COMPANY AT THE ROYAL COURT THEATRE

The English Stage Company was formed to bring serious writing back to the stage. The Court's first Artistic Director, George Devine, wanted to create a vital and popular theatre. In order to promote this, he encouraged new writing that explored subjects drawn from contemporary life as well as pursuing European plays and forgotten classics. When John Osborne's **Look Back in Anger** was first produced in 1956, and revived in '57, it forced British Theatre into the modern age. At the same time Brecht, Giraudoux, Ionesco and Sartre were also part of the repertoire.

The ambition to discover new work which was challenging, innovative and also of the highest quality became the fulcrum of the Company's course of action. Early Court writers included Arnold Wesker, John Arden, David Storey, Ann Jellicoe, N F Simpson and

Edward Bond. They were followed by a generation of writers led by David Hare and Howard Brenton, and in more recent years, celebrated house writers have included Caryl Churchill, Timberlake Wertenbaker, Robert Holman and Jim Cartwright. Many of their plays are now regarded as modern classics.

In line with the policy of nurturing new writing, the Theatre Upstairs has mainly been seen as a place for exploration and experiment, where writers learn and develop their skills prior to the demands of the Main stage auditorium. Anne Devlin, Andrea Dunbar, Sarah Daniels, Jim Cartwright, Clare McIntyre, Winsome Pinnock, and more recently Martin Crimp have, or will in the future, benefit from this process. The Theatre Upstairs proved its value as a focal point for new work with the production of the Chilean writer Ariel Dorfman's **Death and the Maiden**.

More recently talented young writ as diverse as Jonathan Harv Adam Pernak, Phyllis Nagy association with the Liverp Playhouse) and Gregory Motton association with the Royal Natic Theatre Studio) have been show great advantage in this space.

1991, 1992, and 1993 have be record-breaking years at the b office with capacity houses productions of **Top Girls, Th Birds Alighting on a Field, Fa Healer, Death and the Maiden, Degrees of Separation, King Le Oleanna, Hysteria, Calalcade The Kitchen. Death and the Maic and Six Degrees of Separati** won the Olivier Award for Best F in 1992 and 1993 respectiv **Three Birds Alighting on a F** was awarded Best West End Play the Writer's Guild of Great Britai **Hysteria** won 1994's Olivier Aw for Best Comedy.

After nearly four decades, the R Court Theatre is still a major foc the country for the production of work. Scores of plays first see Sloane Square are now part of National and International dram repertoire.

Photo: Ivan Kyncl

Arnold Wesker's **The Kitchen**

THE OLIVIER BUILDING APPEAL

The Royal Court reached the ripe old age of 100 in September 1988. The theatre was showing its age somewhat, and the centenary was celebrated by the launch of the Olivier Appeal, for £800,000 to repair and improve the building.

Laurence Olivier's long association with the Court began as a schoolboy. He was given "a splendid seat in the Dress Circle" to see his first Shakespeare, *Henry IV Part 2* and was later to appear as Malcolm in *Macbeth* (in modern dress) in a Barry Jackson production, visiting from the Birmingham Repertory Theatre in 1928. His line of parts also included the Lord in the Prologue of *The Taming of the Shrew*. This early connection and his astonishing return in *The Entertainer*, which changed the direction of his career in 1957, made it natural that he should be the Appeal Patron. After his death, Joan Plowright CBE, the Lady Olivier, consented to take over as Patron.

We are now in sight of our target. With the generous gifts of our many friends and donors, and an award from the Arts Council's Incentive Fund, we have enlarged and redecorated the bars and front of house areas, installed a new central heating boiler and new air conditioning equipment in both theatres, rewired many parts of the building, redecorated the dressing rooms and we are gradually upgrading the lighting and sound equipment.

With the help of the Theatre Restoration Fund, work has now been completed on building a rehearsal room and replacing the ancient roofs. The Foundation for Sport and the Arts provided a grant which enabled us to restore the faded Victorian facade of the theatre. So, much is being done, but much remains to do, to improve the technical facilities backstage which will open up new possibilities for our set designers.

Can you help? A tour of the theatre, including its more picturesque parts, can be arranged by ringing Catherine King on *071 730 5174*. If you would like to help with an event or a gift please ring Graham Cowley, General Manager, on the same number.
'Secure the Theatre's future, and take it forward towards the new century. For the health of the whole theatrical life of Britain it is essential that this greatly all-providing theatre we love so much and wish so well continues to prosper.'

Laurence Olivier (1988)

Lawrence Olivier 1907-1989
Photo: Snowdon

THE ROYAL COURT THEATRE

We would like to thank the following for their help with this production:

Wreaths made by Mrs J Sheehan at The Flower Box, Hythe Green
The 'Queens' dress made by Martin Taylor
Keith Bolton at Regents Park
Hampstead Theatre
The Bush Theatre
Thanks to BT plc
Coca-Cola Great Britain
Guinness Brewing GB
Marks & Spencer plc
J Sainsbury plc
Waitrose
Trolley supplied by Kwik Save plc
Register supplied by NES Arnold
Tuba supplied by Phil Parker
Oboe case supplied by Howarth's London
Rollerblades supplied by Ealing Sports Centre
Cheese supplied by Kraft Jacobs Suchard
Twiglets suplied by Jacobs plc
Independant Cordless Styler supplied by Braun UK
Kingsmill bread kindly donated by Allied Bakeries
Microwave Popcorn supplied by Golden Valley Microwave Food Inc., manufacturers of 'pop-pop'
     Microwave Popcorn
Cider supplied by The Gaymer Group
Sausage rolls supplied by Pork Farms
Lighters supplied by Rizla Ltd
Football supplied by Umbro

Babies

Characters

Joe Casey	a Learning Support teacher and tutor of 9CY, aged 24
Woody	his boyfriend, aged 26
Vivian Williams	aged 32
Manda Williams	Viv's daughter, aged 16
Tammy Williams	Viv's daughter, a member of 9CY, aged 13
Kenny Figaro	Viv's brother, aged 30
Ivy Williams	Viv's mother-in-law, aged 65
Sonia Sweeney	Viv's next door neighbour and best friend, aged 40
Ernie Sweeney	Sonia's husband, aged 43
Gemma Sweeney	their daughter, aged 14
Kelly	a member of 9CY, aged 14
David	a member of 9CY, aged 14
Richard	a member of 9CY, aged 14
Simone	a member of 9CY, aged 14
Valerie Pinkney	Viv's neighbour over the road, aged 42
Drag Queen	a friend of Kenny's, aged 50

The play is set in south east London, 1994. All the characters who live on the estate speak with South East London accents, whereas Joe and Woody are both from Liverpool. The Drag Queen is from North London.

When the party is in full swing, the music should reflect the taste of the kids, 1994 summer chart music, except when Vivian is playing her Dolly Parton tape.

Act One

Scene One

Classroom

9CY's tutor base, in a modern south east London comprehensive school. There is a teacher's desk and the front row of four students' desks and chairs. At these desks sit **Kelly**, **Simone**, **David** *and* **Richard**. *Their backs are to the audience. Supposedly the rest of the class are where the audience are, so when a character talks or looks to the audience, they are in fact addressing another classmate.*

On the teacher's desk sits **Joe Casey**, *taking the register. He is the form tutor.*

The kids are dressed in modern school uniform: navy blue trousers, sweatshirt and trainers. They each have a 'Head' bag, in different colours, except **Kelly**, *who has a plastic bag.* **David** *also has an oboe case. They are all about thirteen/fourteen.*

Joe Casey *wears jeans and a leather jacket, he is twenty-four. Whereas the kids all speak in broad south east London accents,* **Joe** *speaks with a broad Liverpool twang.*

As **Joe** *takes the register there are various replies of 'here', 'yeah', and 'yo Sir' from the class.* **Simone** *swings round in her chair and chats with her mate* **Angel**, *behind her.*

Joe	Kelly	*At the same time.*
	Lee	
	Donna	**Simone** (*whisper*) Angel! Angel!
	Kellie	Did you see him? . . .
	Lee	What d'he say?
	Simon	Did you tell him? Was he gutted?
	Angel	Are you? . . .
	Lee-Anne	Sit on our bench in science. I
	Terry	wanna know everything. Yeah . . .

Osman	Oh no he didn't! . . .
David	Have you seen Lee-Anne Bennet's
Richard	culottes? . . .
Kelly-Ann	I know! . . .
Sukhvinder	Mark One or what?
Balvinder	(*Laughs.*)
Simone. Simone?	Who give you that black eye?

Simone What? Oh here Sir.

Joe Face the front Simone.

Simone (*tuts*) Tell me in science. (*Turning.*) Yeah Sir.

Joe Kaylee
Justin
Leah
Gurjit
Vicki
Robert
Wayne
and Tammy. Oh yeah. (*Closes register.*) Actually, eyes front 9CY. You too, Balvinder. Right, a word, please. (*Burps.*) Pardon me.

Simone Better out than in.

Joe Thanks Simone. Now. I want yous all to cast your minds back, if you will, to the end of last term. Yeah? Remember that day I sent Tammy on the errand with the staple gun? And I told you all her dad was really ill with cancer? Mm? Well you've probably noticed, but Tammy's not been in school this week.

Kelly (*to* **Simone**) Her dad's died.

Simone Has he?

Joe Well most of you probably know by now, but Tammy's dad died at the weekend.

Kelly Sir. Simone's crying.

Joe Okay.

Kelly (*to* **Simone**) Do it louder. (**Simone***'s crying gets louder.*)

Joe Now when Tammy comes back to school, how d'you think we should all behave? Bearing in mind that her dad's just died.

David Sir, be dead nice and that.

Richard Shut up Simone!

Joe Yeah. Be supportive to her. That's a really important word, yeah? Support. I mean just imagine how you'd feel if your dad had just died, or your mum . . . or your guardian . . . I know I'd be dead sad. So. (*Beat.*) No Balvinder, you wouldn't be over the moon. Balvinder! (*Class giggles.*) Now look here, if I catch any of yous taking the mickey, I'll send you straight to Miss Sterry and we'll see what she's got to say shall we?

Richard She's a lesbian!

Joe Thank you Richard.

Kelly Is she Sir?

Richard She's a moany old cow!

Joe Er excuse me! We don't, and I repeat *don't* talk like that about members of staff in this room, do we?

Richard *tuts.*

Joe Do we?

Richard No Sir.

Joe Thank you. Sexuality is a private and personal thing. Okay? Now a word about your homeworks please, that was the worksheet: 'Cinderella Fights Back'.

Kelly Sir can I take Simone to the toilet?

Joe Er . . .

Kelly Her mascara's run.

Joe Give us your diary.

Simone *goes in her bag for her school diary. She takes out twenty Bensons and a lighter and slips them in her pocket. She then finds her* *diary.* **Kelly** *has jumped out of her seat. She goes and links arms with* **Joe**.

Kelly Ah cheers Sir. In'e a blinding teacher eh?

Joe (*releasing her arm*) What's the rule on physical contact?

Kelly (*tuts*) Ah but you are Sir. I'm glad we never got that Mr Burgess as a tutor, he's real moany.

David It was sad about Freddy Mercury, wannit Sir?

Joe Very, David. Now . . .

David He was gay, wann'e Sir.

Joe I think he was bisexual actually David.

Richard What's that then?

Simone (*getting up with diary*) AC/DC, swings both ways.

Kelly That one out of Erasure's a gayboy, and he's gorgeous!

Simone (*handing diary to* **Joe**) Oh don't Kell! He wears girls' clothes.

Richard I hate fucking poufters!

David Oh Rich!

Kelly You're probably one yourself Rich, tell him Sir.

Joe I'm telling no one nothing. Richard? Would you like to get my magic pen and go and rub out one of your red squares on the merit mark chart? We don't have language or homophobia like that in these four walls. Okay?

Richard Oh that's out of order!

David Haha! Gutted Rich!

Kelly Blinding. Sir!

Joe If you think it's out of order Richard, perhaps you better go and tell Miss Sterry that.

Richard (*as class laughs*) What, that lesbian? (*More laughter.*)

Joe Right. Outside now!

Richard She wears men's clothes!

Joe I said outside!

Richard (*going*) Aw, this school's an arsehole.

Joe You can only judge an arsehole by the turds that pass through it Richard. Get out! (*He goes.*) Right. Now can I talk about your homeworks, which I might add was the most disastrous pile o'crap I've read in me life.

He opens **Simone**'s *diary. Just then seven warning pips sound, heralding the end of registration. Sounds of pandemonium breaking out.*

Joe Oh why are there never enough minutes in the day? Okay, pack your things up and get off to science. I'll have that chat this afternoon.

Simone Sir, me diary Sir.

Joe Pop to the loo on your way to science Simone.

Kelly Oh write us a note to say we'll be late Sir!

Joe I'll do no such thing, now go on.

Kelly God!

Simone I'm changing tutors!

Kelly So am I!

Kelly *and* **Simone** *grab their stuff and go.* **David** *gathers up his bag and oboe case and hangs about until the rest of the class has gone.*

David Sir? I've been picked to be Chelsea's mascot on the thirteenth of June.

Joe Goway have yer?

David Yeah! And guess where we're going!

Joe Where?

David It's an away game, go on, guess!

Joe I . . .

David Liverpool!

Joe Oh well look out for me mother then, she goes to all the home games.

David I'm too old to be mascot really, so me dad told em I was only twelve. He only got away with it coz I'm small.

Joe Good things come in little packages.

David I just hope I don't grow too much before then. I'll be in the shit well and truly. Oh sorry Sir.

Joe What?

David I swore.

Joe Oh yeah, well don't.

David Should I take the register back for ya?

Joe D'you mind?

David No. I gotta put me oboe back in the school safe, it's on the way. See ya Sir.

Joe Cheers David.

David *takes the register and goes to the door. He stops.*

David You aint forgot you still got Richard outside have you Sir?

Joe Er no.

David Should I tell him to come in? Or d'you wanna leave it 'til break time?

Joe Erm . . . break time.

David Staff room? Or are you doing a break duty?

Joe Er . . .

David It's Wednesday Sir, break duty. I'll tell him to see you by the special-needs huts shall I?

Joe Okay.

David Right. Later Sir. (*Going.*) Ere Rich!

David *exits.* **Joe** *packs up his stuff and follows suit.*

Scene Two

Crematorium

It starts to snow. 'You'll Never Walk Alone' sung by a squeaky soprano with electric organ plays out over a tannoy in the grounds of the crematorium. A line of wreaths stands alongside a gravel path. Each wreath has a card with message attached to it. One wreath spells 'Scottie'. Another forms a neck-high bottle of vodka. Another forms a huge packet of 'Marlboro' with a cigarette jutting out.

Viv Williams *and her two daughters* **Manda** *and* **Tammy** *slowly process out of the crematorium. The girls are crying and* **Viv** *walks between them hugging them.* **Viv** *is an attractive thirty-two, young-looking enough to pass for the girls' elder sister.* **Manda** *is sixteen and* **Tammy** *thirteen. They are wrapped up warm to brave the elements.*

Following closely behind them are their next door neighbours **Sonia** *and* **Ernie Sweeney.** *They are all dressed in funeral clothes.* **Sonia** *tries to act and speak a bit classier than* **Viv.**

They stop by the wreaths. **Sonia** *and* **Ernie** *stand apart from the others.* **Ernie** *gets a packet of cigarettes out and offers one to* **Viv.**

Ernie Viv?

Viv *shakes her head.* **Sonia** *stands admiring the bottle of vodka wreath.*

Sonia Isn't that beautiful?

She leans over to read the card attached to it.

Sonia (*reads*) Up in heaven a star is shining
         Down on earth my heart is whining
         Save a place at Jesu's table
         I'll be with you when I'm able.

Tammy I wrote that.

Sonia (*still reading*) Enjoy the vodka, all my love. Tammy.

Manda Read my one Sonia, the packet o'Marlboro.

Sonia (*bends down and reads*) Simply the best
         Better than all the rest

> Better than anyone else
> Anyone I've ever met.
> That's you dad. Love Manda.

Viv His favourite song.

Ernie That's touching that is.

Sonia (*to* **Tammy** *and* **Manda**) Your daddy will be a very proud man.

Viv Right, they've got your nan in the car. You be okay in the second car Son?

Sonia (*nods*) See you back at the house.

Viv (*to girls*) Come on.

She leads off. **Tammy** *wants to stay.* **Manda** *goes back to her, puts her arms round her, hugs her then they go off.* **Sonia** *and* **Ernie** *watch.*

Ernie Automatic.

Sonia What?

Ernie Them cars.

Sonia Where's Gemma?

Ernie Over there reading the tombs.

Sonia Go and get her.

Ernie Shout her.

Sonia Decorum Ernie.

Ernie *goes off to fetch their daughter.* **Valerie Pinkney** *comes along the gravel path with a small arrangement of flowers. She adds it to the line of wreaths.*

Sonia Valerie, I didn't realise you were here.

Valerie Didn't cry did she?

Sonia Vivian?

Valerie When my Norman passed on I was inconsolable.

Sonia She'd had half a tranquiliser off Doctor Nayar.

Valerie Them cars is a bit common. It's the girls I feel sorry for.

Ernie *returns.*

Ernie Says she's staying here.

Valerie I'm expected at the washeteria.

Valerie *goes off.*

Sonia What's she staying here for?

Ernie Says she likes it.

Sonia Oh I've got some cherry lips in my pocket. You go and stall the car. I'll go and coax her.

Ernie *goes off one way,* **Sonia** *the other.*

Sonia Gemma?

'Simply the Best' by Tina Turner, starting at the chorus, bursts out leading us into the next scene.

Scene Three

Street

On the same estate as the school, six months later.

Vivian Williams *and her two daughters,* **Manda** *and* **Tammy**, *career down the pavement.* **Viv** *is smoking, and pushing a Kwik-Save trolley piled high with bags of food. They carry shopping bags.* **Tammy** *jumps on the side of the trolley to try and have a ride on it. They are now all dressed in summery gear.*

Viv (*slapping her off*) Oi, get down from there Tammy!

Manda Act your age, Camel tits.

Tammy *comes off, but almost immediately jumps on again.* **Viv** *slaps her across the hands, forcing her down.*

Viv Get down Tammy! How many times d'you need telling? It'll buckle under your weight.

Manda Fat slag!

Tammy Piss off!

Viv stops the trolley, slaps **Tammy** *across the bum and then points at her in the face, intimidatingly, all three actions well rehearsed, and very fast.*

Viv Oi!! You've got a fat arse! I've told you. (*Points to trolley.*) Now push!

Tammy (*tuts*) God.

They move off again. **Tammy** *pushes the trolley a lot slower than her mum.*

Viv Hurry up girl, we haven't got all day!

Viv *and* **Manda** *laugh.* **Viv** *passes the ciggie over the trolley to a grateful* **Manda**, *who has a few drags.*

Tammy It's heavy.

Viv Well use your bloody elbow grease.

Tammy I'm pushing as hard as I can!

Manda Well push harder! (*Passes ciggie back to* **Viv**.)

Tammy Carry some more bags Manda.

Manda Libs!

Tammy Shut up.

Manda (*putting her own bags in the trolley*) Haha gutted! Wait 'til the Pinkneys see you!

Tammy The Pinkneys are a bunch of slags!

Viv Watch out for that dog crap Tam.

Tammy Me arm hurts.

Viv It's your birthday Tammy. You gotta do something towards it.

Tammy I'll do the hoover.

Viv Manda's doing that.

Manda Oh libs!

Viv Shut up and talk properly Manda. You're as bad as her.

Manda Well none of my mates are coming to this bloody party. Not even me own bloody boyfriend.

Viv Yeah well when your bloody boyfriend can see his way clear to being bloody civil to me he can step back inside our house. I don't like him.

Tammy Gutted! Haha!

Manda Fat arse!

Viv Oi! Don't start.

Tammy What time's Kenny coming then?

Viv He's bringing your nan round about eight.

Manda Oh God.

Tammy Is she still coming?

Viv She's still your nan, Tammy, even if your dad has died.

Tammy And is Kenny staying?

Viv No. He's gotto open the pub up ann'e? But he'll be back later on.

Manda He is coming though?

Viv Yes! Any more questions?

They slow down as they reach the Pinkneys' house. They stop and stare in the direction of the audience, standing in front of the trolley so that it is hidden from view.

Viv Aye aye. The Pinkneys are in.

Manda State of their windows. You'd think they could see 'emselves clear to getting 'em mended.

Tammy (*sings, like a football chant*) Trampo-os! Trampo-os!

Viv Who's she looking at?

Manda Gozzy bitch.

Viv (*shouts*) Yeah you can stare Valerie Pinkney! Oh yeah? Yeah? (*To girls.*) Look at her shaking her head. (*Shouts.*) It's only shopping, Valerie! (*They step aside to reveal the trolley.*) No law against that. It's bloody paid for! (*To girls.*) Over the road and in.

The three of them retreat to the back of the stage. **Viv** *gets a key out of her pocket and hands it to* **Manda**. **Manda** *and* **Tammy** *start unloading the trolley and exit.*

Viv Everything straight in the kitchen.

Viv *hasn't taken her eyes off* **Valerie Pinkney**'s *house.* **Tammy** *and* **Manda** *exit.* **Manda** *comes back with an envelope.*

Manda There's another letter here mum.

Viv Give it here.

Manda *hands her mum the letter and looks to* **Valerie Pinkney**. **Viv** *holds the letter up and rips it for* **Valerie** *to see. She then sticks a finger up and exits with some shopping bags.* **Manda** *follows.*

Scene Four

Joe Casey's *lounge*

An old wooden ironing board with an iron on it stands next to a comfy chair. Sprawled across the chair is **Joe Casey**'s *fella* **Woody**. *He flicks through the channels on TV with a remote control and settles on watching 'Blind Date'.* **Joe** *comes in holding two shirts on coat hangers.* **Woody** *has a Liverpool accent too.*

Joe Which d'you think? (*Pause.*) I'm talking to you.

Pause. **Woody** *shifts round in his seat to look at* **Joe**.

Woody What?

Joe Which d'you think?

Woody Well it depends, doesn't it?

Joe On what?

Woody On whether you wanna be the Butch Skal or the Camp Queen.

Joe Oh the Butch Skal, definitely the Butch Skal.

Woody Well neither then, you'll have to take something of mine.

Joe (*not giving up*) Woody, which one?

Woody I don't want anything to do with this and you know that.

Joe I'll wear this.

He drapes one shirt over the back of the easy chair and sets about ironing the other.

Joe Are you going out tonight?

Pause. **Woody** *pretends not to hear.*

Joe (*to himself, but for* **Woody** *to hear*) Oh! I'm having a relationship with Helen Keller.

Woody Might go to the Fridge.

Joe Oh might yer?

Woody Yeah I might, coz Paul rang and he's going.

Joe Oh that's nice for yer.

Woody Yeah and it'll be nice for all the other Liverpool queens who are going an' all.

Joe Oh you'll have a ball then.

Woody Yeah, I will. If I go.

Joe God, what's to do with this iron? Have you been ironing your shell suit bottoms again?

Woody I'd be justified.

Joe It's just one night Woody. All the nights I've sat in here, staring at Cilla Black, knowing you're on a bender and won't be back 'til Sunday tea-time . . . how d'you think that makes me feel?

Woody You don't like E.

Joe I don't like relying on it to make me feel everything's okay.

Woody Oh and I do?

Joe There must be some reason why you do it.

Pause. **Joe** *carries on ironing.* **Woody** *starts emptying his pockets out, looking for something.*

Woody Where's me Rizlas? Have you moved me Rizlas?

Joe Oh, starting early tonight aren't we? What's it to be then? A little later on . . . eh? Two Es? Three Es? Six?

Woody Twenty-five the way you're making me feel!

Joe Yeah well not on my wages, mate! If you can't sort your head out Woody, and I know I can't, don't run away to drugs to help yer.

Woody I haven't for the past three weekends!

Joe So why go back now?

Woody All I want is a joint. You've never batted an eyelid about a joint before.

Joe It's not the joints I'm worried about Woody, it's you.

Woody Well don't go to this fucking kid's party then. That wasn't part o'the deal.

Joe Woody, we've been through all this. I've got to know the family, haven't I? Since the dad died. Show some respect for God's sake.

Woody I wouldn't've been seen dead inviting one o'my teachers to a party. That girl must be seriously off her chunk!

Joe Ah well you never had a teacher like me did yer?

Woody Can't I come with yer?

Joe You're the one who kept going on about space.

Woody *turns the TV off with the remote. He fingers the shirt on the back of the chair a while.*

Woody What are you like eh? Six months ago you were moaning on at me to tell me ma and da . . . an' all that . . . and now look at you. Going round there and pretending you're straight.

Joe You were so far back in the closet you were in fucking Narnia.

Woody I told them didn't I?

Joe I know lad.

Woody D'you just not mention it or what?

Joe Yeah.

Woody Well . . . what if they say have you got a bird?

Joe Can't keep pets in this flat, simple as that.

Woody (*correcting himself*) Girlfriend.

Joe I don't know.

Woody Ah you're doing me head in Joey.

Joe Oh and what d'you want me to say? Well actually I live with an electrician called Woody who gooses me twice nightly?

Woody Twice nightly? Don't flatter yourself.

Joe Can you imagine the sort of stick you'da given your teachers if you'd known they were gay?

Pause. **Woody** *switches the TV back on.* **Joe**'*s still ironing.*

Woody You're gonna kill me if I do E tonight aren't yer?

Joe No.

Pause.

Joe Just don't expect me to go traipsing halfway round London tomorrow trying to find you. If you forget where you live again Woody then go and chill out at Paul's. (*Beat.*) And fucking stay there.

Woody *gets up out of the chair and makes for the door.* **Joe** *puts the iron down.*

Joe Where are you goin'?

Woody I'm goin' out!

Joe I didn't mean it Wood!

Woody Well why say it then? (*Makes to go again.*)

Joe Woody!

Woody (*stops*) What?

Joe You haven't even changed!

Woody Doesn't matter what I'm wearing! Three hours from now these rags'll be fucking silk mate I'm telling yer! Fucking silk!

Woody *runs out. A door bangs.* **Joe** *slowly makes his way back to the iron and recommences ironing.*

Scene Five

Street

Valerie Pinkney *is out sweeping her path. She's early forties, hair up in a pineapple effect and wearing an England football club tracksuit and Scholls. She sweeps fiercely at the letter which* **Viv** *ripped up earlier, every so often having a look at* **Viv**'s *house.*

Outside **Viv**'s *house stands the empty shopping trolley. Suddenly* **Viv**'s *front door opens and* **Tammy** *comes out. She gets the trolley and begins crossing the street, pushing the empty trolley back to the supermarket.*

Valerie Child labour's illegal in Britain!

Tammy Stop writing letters to my mum!

Valerie Your mother oughta be ashamed of herself!

Tammy Stop putting them through our door.

Valerie I saw the drink in that trolley. Street smells like a brewery thanks to her!

Tammy Dad died six months ago now!

Valerie Six months is nothing!

Tammy She's entitled to enjoy herself!

Valerie Your dad'd turn in his grave if he knew how she carries on. In at all hours, carrying on . . .

Tammy You didn't know my dad like . . .

Valerie He was my bus driver! An upstanding pillar he was. Sixteen years he took me to work!

Tammy Shame he never crashed!

Valerie Ooh the conker dunt fall far from the tree.

Tammy Piss off.

Valerie (*holds brush like a spear*) Come here and say that, lady!

Tammy It's all right.

Tammy *moves off.* **Valerie** *shakes the brush after her.*

Valerie Go on!

Tammy I'm going!

Valerie Go on!

Tammy *goes off with the trolley.* **Valerie** *attacks her path with gusto. Just then,* **Viv**'s *next door neighbour* **Sonia** *pops her head out of an upstairs window.*

Sonia Tammy!?!

Tammy *stops and looks up. So does* **Valerie**.

Sonia Evening Valerie.

Valerie *grunts and goes back indoors with her brush.*

Tammy What?

Sonia Can you give my front door a good push? Only it's stuck and I gotta get round to do your mum's hair. You give it a push and I'll come down and try pulling. Don't go away.

Sonia's *head disappears.*

Scene Six

Viv's *bedroom*

There is a double bed and a dressing table stool. **Viv** *sits on the dressing table stool while her mate from next door,* **Sonia**, *tongs her hair with a Braun Independent.* **Sonia** *is forty, and carries specs on a chain round her neck.* **Manda** *sits on the bed, holding a letter from* **Valerie Pinkney** *open in her hand.*

Manda How d'you spell prostitute?

Sonia P.R.O.S.

Viv T.I.T.

Sonia U.T.E. init?

Viv Mmh.

Manda Cor her spelling's diabolical.

Sonia Takes one to know one I say. D'you know what I mean Vivian?

Viv I do Sonia. Carry on Mand.

Manda (*reads letter*) 'Your Scottie was a decent man. If he wasn't dead now, he'd have topped himself with the shame you're making of his good name.'

Sonia Ooh!

Manda 'The thing that makes me most angry . . .'

Viv Listen to this bit . . .

Manda 'Is what it's doing to your poor girls. Your Manda and your Tammy.'

Sonia As if you didn't know what their names were. D'you know what I mean Vivian?

Viv Mmh!

Manda 'A little bird tells me they've both been seen down the Sewage.'

Viv I hope you haven't, Missis!

Manda (*tuts*) No! She's a lying old cow.

Sonia Carry on love.

Manda (*reading*) 'You're a tramp, a whore and a hussy Vivian Williams and your dress sense leaves a lot to be desired. You're not fit to be a mother. And I won't stop 'til the pair of them are put in a home.'

Sonia Write a letter to the council. That's harassment that is. Give her a taste of her own medicine, I say. Get her transferred.

Viv If I don't deck her first.

Sonia Where does violence get you Viv? Fourteen Nowhere Street, that's where. You wanna keep every letter she writes as evidence.

Viv You get ready now Mand.

Manda I'm talking wi'yous two.

Viv No you're not, get ready.

Manda (*tuts, gets up*) I hate living here.

Viv Well move out then. I could do with the space.

Manda (*tuts*) I will.

Sonia Hard life, init Manda?

Manda No. (*Exits.*)

Sonia She's at that age, isn't she?

Viv What, when they're a little bitch all the time?

Sonia Mm.

Viv She's always been that age.

Sonia *continues to tong* **Viv***'s hair. Her hand starts to shake.*

Sonia I'm getting a flashback Viv!

Viv What? On the bed. Sit on the bed.

Sonia Ooh! (*Sits.*)

Viv Describe it to me Sonia. I'll get me pad. Hang on.

Sonia It's her. Oh God! She's come for me again. I don't want to go.

Viv What's she saying Sonia? I'm right there with you babes.

Sonia I can't hear. It's too noisy.

Viv Try Sonia.

Sonia She's saying 'Come, little girl, come with me.'

Viv No!

Sonia Yeah!

Viv *has a notepad out from under the bed. She scribbles in it as* **Sonia** *speaks.*

Viv Keep going Sonia.

Sonia It's dark. Who turned the light out?

Viv Brilliant!

Sonia No . . . no . . .

Viv Concentrate Sonia.

Sonia No . . . it's going.

Viv Concentrate!

Sonia (*tuts*) No. (*The flashback has ended.*)

Viv Oh that was short, wannit?

Sonia Mm. Ooh I feel all dirty.

Viv Few more like that and the *News of the World* are gonna love you!

Sonia Why does it always happen when I'm not feeling hundred percent?

Viv That's when you're susceptible Sonia. (*Puts pad under bed.*) That's when the spirit world strikes.

Sonia Oh I coulda done without that.

Viv Come on. Finish me off then I'll do you.

Sonia (*tuts*) I dunno.

Sonia *gets up and starts tonging* **Viv**'s *hair again.*

Viv So what's wrong? Your back again?

Sonia I'll be on edge all night. In case any of them kids bash into me.

Viv I'll warn 'em Sonia.

Sonia I wanna come, don't get me wrong. It's just . . . well we couldn't afford a party this year for our Gemma. She was ever so upset.

Viv Well what's a birthday without a party?

Sonia That's what I say.

Viv But you're working now. You can give her a blinding one at Christmas.

Sonia I know. I know. She's going round with such a face on her. It gets me down.

Viv Has she started?

Sonia No it's not that. They took her support teacher off of her.

Viv What?

Sonia Last week. I had to go to an appeal.

Viv She needs that support teacher.

Sonia Well they say she don't.

Viv She can't read, Sonia!

Sonia Oh you try telling them that. It's Greenwich Education init? Buggered in my book.

Viv She was nice that support teacher.

Sonia I know.

Viv Had a look of Moira Stuart.

Sonia I told her.

Viv You wanna tell Joe. See if he can sort something out.

Sonia Joe?

Viv Tammy's teacher. He's coming tonight.

Sonia Oh.

Viv Tammy thinks the world of him.

Sonia I think it's too late.

Viv No! He can work wonders that Joe. When Tammy flooded the school toilets playing silly buggers with her mates, he got us off paying the bill.

Sonia Oh?

Viv Yeah. Told that Miss Sterry one we were in unfortunate circumstances, what with Scottie and that.

Sonia Oh they wanna have more teachers like that, I say.

Viv Have a chat with him. You never know. He's quite tasty as it happens.

Sonia Viv!

Viv What?

Sonia You're awful you are.

Viv I'm a single woman.

Sonia Oh I'm saying nothing.

Viv Sing my praises to him Sonia. That's all.

Sonia You wanna be careful?

Viv Since when have I ever been careful?

Sonia He might be a married man.

Viv No. He's young. Healthy.

Sonia Well, a bird in the hand's worth two in the bush, I say. That's you done. Give it a brush.

Viv *steps up and brushes her hair through.*

Viv Brilliant Sonia. You're an angel.

Sonia Dunno bout that. (*Sits on stool.*) Make it simple, I gotta feed the dog.

Viv *takes the tongs to* **Sonia**'s *hair.*

Scene Seven

Viv's *lounge*

A music centre blares out 'All That She Wants' by Ace of Base. In a cosy armchair in the corner sits **Manda**, *having a fag. She is now dressed for the party, wearing a blue blazer of her mother's with the sleeves rolled back, a bra top, cycling shorts and high heels. Her hair is lacquered and frizzed to high heaven, and she has slapped the make-up on. Her legs are crossed and she gyrates her foot in time to the music.*

Elsewhere in the room is a low coffee table and a trolley, both piled high with food. A sheepskin rug lies on the floor. Next to **Manda**'s *armchair stands an occasional table with a photo of her late father on it. Finally, three high bar stools are placed around the room.*

Tammy *enters with a tray of sausage rolls. She too is dicky-dolled-up for the party, in a short, dusty pink PVC raincoat, humungous gold ear-rings and spanking new trainers. On her hands she wears fingerless lace gloves. Her hair is gelled close to her head in a ballerina bun at the back.*

Manda What are they?

Tammy Sausage rolls.

Manda Coffee table.

Tammy *puts the tray down on the trolley.*

Manda I said coffee table!

Tammy Shut up!

Manda If you put 'em on the trolley it'll fuckin' break won't it? You stupid cow.

Tammy *takes the tray and puts it on the coffee table instead.*

Manda Hurry up, people are gonna start arriving soon.

Tammy *tuts and exits.* **Manda** *flicks her ash extravagantly onto the carpet, still gyrating to the music. Presently* **Tammy** *comes back in with a second tray.* **Tammy** *puts it on the coffee table.*

Manda What you doin' now?

Tammy What's it look like?

Manda Put 'em on the trolley, now!

Tammy Why?!

Manda Just do it will ya?

Tammy You told me to put the sausage rolls on the coffee table!

Manda Yeah, but they're not sausage rolls, they're sandwiches. Sandwiches int as heavy as sausage rolls. Wor! Was you born a moron?!

Tammy (*tuts*) God!

Tammy *does as she is told then makes her way out of the room as* **Viv** *enters, boogieing. She wears a figure-hugging leopard-skin fun-fur dress, black high heels, a gold bow in her hair and an ankle chain. She is carrying a spritzer and a lit cigarette. She looks dressed to kill.*

Viv Go and help Tammy, Manda.

Manda Why?

Viv Coz you'll feel the back o'my hand if you don't.

Manda Who says I'm coming to this bloody party anyway?

Viv Your clothes have got party written all over 'em.

Manda My clothes have got my bloke written all over 'em. (*Points to a different item of clothing as she spells his name.*) S.I.D.D.I.E. Siddie!

Viv *goes and smacks* **Manda** *once over the head.*

Viv Kitchen. Now.

Manda (*tuts*) Didn't hurt.

Viv *smacks her again.* **Manda** *winces, then starts bouffing up her hair.* **Viv** *goes over to the music centre and switches tapes. Dolly Parton's 'Potential New Boyfriend' comes on.* **Manda** *voluntarily gets up and goes out. The doorbell goes.* **Viv** *is too busy boogieing to answer it.*

Kenny, **Viv**'*s brother, comes in, wheeling* **Ivy** *in a wheelchair. He is about thirty, wears a white T-shirt with the sleeves rolled back, displaying chunks of tanned bicep.* **Ivy** *is sixty-five, and wears a mauve terry-towelling tracksuit and slippers. She has gold jewellery draped about her person.*

Viv Oright Kenny?

Kenny Where should I stick her?

Viv In the corner. I'll give you an 'and.

Kenny We'll stick you in that chair Ivy.

Viv Next to the photo of Scottie.

Kenny In case you get bored.

Viv Okay Ivy?

Kenny Let's lift you up.

They wheel her to the corner of the room and get her out of the wheelchair.

Viv Cor, you aint half put on weight Ive.

They put her in the chair.

Kenny Happy now Ivy?

Viv She's all right. Look at her she's in cloud-cuckoo-land.

Kenny (*indicating wheelchair*) Where d'you want this?

Viv Under the stairs.

Kenny *wheels the chair out.* **Manda** *enters with a big cake.* **Viv** *starts boogieing again, in front of* **Ivy**.

Viv D'you like this one mum?

Manda *puts the cake down on the coffee table.*

Viv It's Dolly. You like Dolly don't you? Yes.

Manda The icing's a different colour.

Viv We'll get you up dancing later Ive.

Manda From where you took the lettering off.

Viv (*to* **Manda**) Don't start.

Manda The lettering that said Merry Christmas.

Viv Shut up about Christmas cake, it's still fresh.

Manda You better not give me a Christmas cake for me birthday or I'll feel ashamed.

Viv The only cake you'll be getting'll have a file in it. Coz you'll be inside. For cheek.

Manda Libs!

Viv Have you said hello to your Gran?

Manda Yeah, in the hall.

Viv Yeah well talk to her.

Viv *moves back to the rug and keeps boogieing, now singing as well.* **Manda** *reluctantly goes and squats next to* **Ivy**'s *chair. She points at the photo.*

Manda See that Gran? That's dad. That's Scottie. Your son.

Viv Oh don't start her off. You know what she gets like Mand. Go and get her a drink.

Manda Kenny's getting her one.

Viv You're not on tablets are you mum?

Enter **Sonia**, *hair done, same clothes as before.*

Sonia I heard you were here Ivy.

Viv Yeah, worse luck.

Sonia I heard your wheels on the path. Marvellous things, wheelchairs.

Viv Well don't say it to me, say it her.

Sonia You keeping well Ivy? Good.

Sonia *goes and stands in front of* **Ivy**, *talking loudly and deliberately.*

Sonia Here, that's a nice tracksuit Ivy. I'd like a tracksuit like that.

Manda Marvellous things, tracksuits.

Sonia Is that terry towelling?

Manda No, it's me dad!

Sonia I've gotta pop next door Ive, and get me gladrags on.

Viv (*to* **Manda**) Int she blinding eh? (*To* **Sonia**.) You're a bonus to that rest home Son.

Manda Surprised you aint lost your voice by now.

Viv Don't touch Sonia, Manda, she's got bad back.

Manda Don't worry, I wasn't gonna.

Sonia (*to* **Viv**) Okay? I've gotta feed my Brenda. (*To* **Ivy**.) I'll see you later Ivy, have a nice long chat. Okay?

Viv Huh! You'll be lucky. (*As* **Sonia** *exits*.) See you babe.

Sonia See you later, won't be long.

Viv Ciao for now!

Sonia *exits.*

Viv (*to* **Ivy**, *suddenly shouting*) You remember Sonia, don't you mum? Yes. Ivy? Wake her up Mand. Jesus. (*To* **Ivy**.) This is a party Ivy.

Kenny *enters with a drink for* **Ivy**.

Kenny Got you a drink here Ivy.

Viv What you got?

Kenny Light ale.

Viv Hold it for her Mand.

Manda (*tuts*) God, do I have to do everything round here.

Viv (*to* **Kenny**) You getting off then Kenneth?

Kenny Yeah. You get that money?

Viv In me purse. (*Gets purse off table.*) What time you coming back?

Kenny Soon as I can.

Manda Mum can I go the pub with Kenny?

Viv You're staying here Madam.

Manda Oh it's boring here.

Kenny You don't wanna come with me Mand. I got a few things to sort out. You'd be sat in the bar, bored out your skull.

Manda I'm bored out me skull here. She won't even let me own bloke come to the party.

Viv (*handing* **Kenny** *the money*) Twenty, forty, forty-five, fifty.

Kenny (*gets a cassette tape out of his pocket*) Have it ready to play at eleven. Synchronise watches and all that.

Viv Okay. Mand? Mind that for us will you, and don't tell no one.

Manda What is it?

Viv It's a tape, what's it look like?

Manda I'm not blind.

Viv Well don't ask what it is then. Jesus.

Kenny It's a surprise.

Manda (*sarcastic*) Oh I'm holding me breath.

Viv Don't do that, you might die. And don't smoke in front of your Gran, it'll only set her off.

Kenny (*getting off*) Later then, all right?

Viv Come on Ken, I'll show you out.

Viv *and* **Kenny** *exit.* **Manda** *lights another fag and smiles cunningly at* **Ivy**.

Manda D'you want one Gran? (*Laughs.*) Want some o'your drink? It's got acid in it. (*Laughs.*) Oh wake up Gran!

Viv *comes back in, boogieing onto the rug. The doorbell goes.*

Viv I love this rug. You bought us this rug dint you mum?

Manda She's asleep.

Viv Oh sod her then.

Tammy *enters with* **David**. *He wears a Chelsea top, jeans and trainers. His hair is gelled to perfection.* **Tammy** *has opened his card and shows it to* **Viv**.

Tammy Mum, look what David got me.

Viv (*to* **David**) Oh hello Trouble.

Tammy (*the card*) Look it pops up.

Viv Yeah well I hope that's the only thing that does pop up tonight Dave or there'll be bloody murder. I've told her, no one's going in the bedrooms, you can do your funny business on the stairs. Be warned.

Tammy (*tuts*) God.

Viv Go and get your guest a drink Tam.

Tammy He aint a cripple.

Viv What d'you want Dave?

David Can I have a coke please?

Viv Ooh Mr Teetotal! Coke from the kitchen Tammy please. Hurry up.

Tammy (*tuts*) God. (*Going.*)

Viv He's your guest girl.

Tammy All right all right. (*Exits.*)

Viv Dancing Dave?

David David. No thanks.

Viv (*dancing*) Come on, not often you get an offer from an older woman is it?

David No.

Viv Sit on a high stool so I can speak to you. Cor, you in 'alf small.

David (*climbing onto a bar stool*) Good things come in little packages.

Viv (*laughs*) Don't believe a word of it! (*Laughs.*) Ooh wash my mouth out with soap and water! Take no notice of me Dave. I'm what you call a modern mother.

Manda (*tuts*) And the rest.

David Is Mr Casey coming tonight?

Viv (*laughs*) I hope so Dave!

David David. He's an all right teacher as it happens.

Viv You're telling me!

David He's the best teacher there. Listens to you.

Viv 'Ere, you might be able to answer this. Has he got a girlfriend?

David I don't know. Why, is he bringing someone?

Viv I bloody hope not!

David I know he lives up Charlton. And he comes from Liverpool. And he's vegetarian.

Viv Is he? (*Dances over to food.*) Do vegetarians eat cheese?

David I think so.

Viv Cake?

David I woulda thought so.

Manda Christmas cake an' all?

Viv Shut up!

David I don't see why not. He gave us all a card for Christmas, what he'd designed himself. And a candle, a scented candle. I've still got mine.

Viv Tammy set fire to the bloody mattress with that she did.

Tammy *enters with a glass of coke.*

Viv (*to* **Tammy**) You little cow!

Tammy (*tuts*) Here you are David.

David Cheers Tammy.

Tammy Can I change that tape mum?

Viv What, Dolly Parton?

Tammy Yeah.

Viv You telling me no one wants to listen my Dolly?!

Tammy Manda bought me East 17, let me put it on.

Viv Later Tammy, Jesus you're so impatient! Now David, come and meet Tammy's Gran.

David It's all right.

Viv She won't bite. She's got her teeth out.

Tammy She's had three strokes.

Manda Imagine how you'd feel if you'd had three strokes and stumpy gits wouldn't talk to you.

Viv *slaps* **Ivy** *round the chops lightly three times to wake her.* **David** *gets down off his stool and goes over, sipping his drink.*

Viv Ivy? Ivy? This is Dave, one of Tammy's school friends.

David All right?

Viv (*to* **Ivy**) In'e tiny?

Tammy (*tuts*) Mum.

Viv He's so cute I could eat him. Tell her a bit about yourself Dave (*A la Cilla Black.*) What's your name and where d'you come from? (*Laughs.*)

David D'you mind calling me David, Mrs Williams?

Viv Yeah I do, you snotty brat, now talk to her.

David What's her name?

Tammy Nana Williams.

There is a ring at the doorbell. **Viv** *and* **Tammy** *both make a run for it, leaving* **David** *with* **Ivy** *and a very unimpressed* **Manda**.

Tammy I'll get it!

Viv *I'll* get it!

Manda Talk to her, you stumpy prat.

David All right Mrs Williams?

Manda (*tuts*) You gotta do better than that.

David You all right?

Manda (*tuts*) She's had three strokes you silly prick, would you be all right if you'd had three strokes?!

David I don't know.

Manda (*tuts*) Kids! (*Gets up.*) Talk to her!

Manda *exits.* **David** *is left alone with* **Ivy**.

David You know I said my teacher was from Liverpool? Well it's funny, coz right, I was up Liverpool last week. I was! I was Chelsea's mascot. You know when the teams run onto the pitch? Yeah well I had to run on as well, carrying the ball. I was on 'Match of the Day'. Got it on video if you wanna lend it.

Pause.

Trials next week. Charlton Youth Team. Dad says I'll walk it. And mum says I better not walk, I better get the bus! (*Laughs.*)

Pause.

Can you play any musical instruments? I can. I'm having oboe lessons. Got an exam in a month, Grade Two Practical. It's blinding, the oboe. Well better than football. I gotta play a piece called 'Song Without Words'. This is the fingering.

He mimes playing the tune on the oboe. Then stops.

Can you keep a secret? I aint told me dad I'm having oboe lessons. I was gonna, but . . . I paid for the exam with me paper round. See my dad, he says . . . are you asleep?

Pause.

I hate football. Grown out of it see.

Simone, **Kelly**, **Richard** *and* **Tammy** *enter during* **David**'s *last line.* **Kelly** *wears white jeans, a purple NafNaf jacket and trainers. She has a purple bow in her hair and carries a present.* **Simone** *wears a lycra catsuit, high heels, and a leather waistcoat. She carries a massive present.* **Richard** *wears a luminous lime green shell suit, black cap and shades. He carries a pizza box.* **Simone** *has one shoe off and one shoe on. The heel on one of her shoes has come off, and she carries one shoe between her teeth. She takes it out of her mouth as* **David** *finishes his speech.*

Simone (*tuts*) David's pulled.

Kelly He don't waste any time, does he?

David Oh shut up will you? She fought a war for us!

Kelly Yeah and look at the state of her!

Tammy Shut up, that's my gran you're talking about!

David She's had three strokes!

Simone Don't lie!

Tammy She has, so you can shut up an' all. Are they my presents?

Kelly Yeah. Happy Birthday Tammy.

Simone Yeah Tammy. Happy Birthday.

They pass the presents to **Tammy**. **Kelly** *hugs* **Tammy**.

Kelly Oh you're such a good friend Tammy.

Tammy I'll open them on the breakfast bar.

Tammy *exits with the presents.*

Simone You're such a liar Kell.

Kelly So?

Enter **Viv**.

Viv All right kids? (*They all say hello.*) Bloody hell Richard, what have you got on?

Richard Shell suit.

Viv Turn the volume down Rich!

Simone (*to* **Richard**) You got a nob for that?

Viv Is that my pizza love?

Richard Yeah.

Viv (*takes it*) Great. I'll stick on me wotsit. In pride of place. (*Goes to trolley.*) Here, have a sausage roll! (*Laughs.*)

A barrage of sausage rolls comes flying across the room as **Viv** *chucks one to each kid.*

David (*to* **Ivy**) That's Richard, his mum works for Domino Pizzas. That's Kelly.

Kelly My mum's a moany old cow.

David And that's Simone.

Simone All right? (*To* **Kelly**.) I hate old people.

Kelly Stink, dunt they?

Simone I know.

Richard Stink of piss.

Kelly Piss, shit and everything.

Simone Keep away from her.

Kelly Right.

Viv Come through to me kitchen and let's fix you some drinks.

Simone Viv, have you got anything for sticking heels back on shoes?

Viv No.

Simone (*to* **Kelly**) Oh our Sheneel's gonna kill me. She don't even know I've got 'em.

Kelly Don't!

Simone (*to* **Viv**) Superglue'll do.

Viv We got Pritt Stick.

Viv exits. Followed by **Richard**, **Simone** *and* **Kelly**. **David** *is left again with* **Ivy**. *He'd like to go through to the kitchen but feels he shouldn't leave* **Ivy** *alone. He stands like a man in a bar, searching for small talk. He finally finds something to say.*

David Was you alive in the war? This was all marshes, wannit? I know coz me dad told me. Did you have a Anderson shelter? My nan did.

Enter **Joe**, *with a bottle of wine. He wears a ravey get-up and a leather jacket.*

Joe Hiya David.

David All right Sir? Put it there mate. (*They shake hands.*)

Joe The front door was open. (**Ivy**.) All right?

David She's had three strokes init.

Joe Oh aye?

David Sad init?

Joe Ah. Is Tammy's mum around?

David Yeah in the kitchen, I'll show you. Here, that's a blinding top you've got on there Sir. Where d'you get that then, Liverpool?

Joe Er . . . no down here.

David Oh what shop was it? Mighta seen it.

Joe Oh it was up in Soho.

David Oh yeah? Which one?

Joe Oh I don't think you'd know it David.

David Might do.

Joe Clone Zone.

David Mmm, nah. Eh! See you've got your Biffa Bacon boots on! Blinding! I've got a pair like that in the house.

Joe Fab!

David Yeah, you come on through to the kitchen Sir, meet Tammy's mum. After you. Age before beauty, as they say. No offence.

Joe Pearls before swine. (*Exits.*)

David See you later Mrs Williams. Nice talking to you. Enjoy yourself, yeah?

David *exits.* **Ivy** *is left alone. Dolly Parton is still playing. She looks lost.*

Scene Eight

Next door

Sonia *is standing on her landing, outside her daughter* **Gemma**'s *bedroom door. She has changed into a canary yellow dress suit top with gold buttons and a pleated floral skirt. She wears black court shoes with gold buckles. As she talks she is slowly opening a can of dog food with a tin opener.*

Sonia I do wish you'd open this door, Gemma. (*Pause.*) Gemma? (*Pause.*) I know you're in there. Your dad's just phoned. He's stuck in Birmingham. Ah, I don't wanna go on me own love. Not really. I wanna go with you. (*Pause.*) All your friends'll be there. (*Pause.*) What's Tammy going to think? She won't want to come to your party now. Coz you're gonno have one. Now I'm working. And you can have all your friends round. (*Beat.*) Elizabeth, Shirley . . . all the girls from the Special Class. (*Pause.*) Gemma, is it your spots love? (*Pause.*) Everyone gets spots at fourteen. (*Pause.*) I had me flashback before. Wann'alf scary, d'you know what I mean, that woman. Ooh, makes you think dunnit eh? Mmm. (*Pause.*) You've got those nice velvetty leggins. Everyone else'll say. ' 'Ere, look at Gem, she's got nice velvetty leggins, see?' (*Pause.*) Are you gonna come Gemma?

Suddenly, from inside the bedroom, a tuba starts playing loudly. The tune is 'Au Claire de la Lune'. **Sonia** *stares at the door and sighs. She has opened the can.*

Sonia (*shouts*) Well I'm gonna go! I just hope that teacher doesn't report me for leaving you home alone! I'll be massacred!

She starts to walk off, towards her stairs. She waggles the dog food in front of her.

Sonia Brenda?! Brenda! Look what mummy's got you!

She exits.

Scene Nine

Viv's *back patio*

There is a door through to the kitchen, the back door, and a fence next to **Sonia**'s *patio. Out the back are* **Simone**, **Kelly** *and* **Richard**, *having a drinking contest. They count down from ten to zero and then knock back their drinks.* **Kelly** *and* **Simone** *have large spritzers,* **Richard** *has a can of lager.* **Simone** *is now barefoot. Halfway down their glasses, she and* **Kelly** *burst out laughing and spit their* *drinks out.* **Richard,** *laughing, isn't deterred, finishing off the whole can.*

Simone Cor how d'you do it Rich?

Richard Dunno!

Richard *staggers about a bit to entertain the girls. The three of them have a bit of a laugh, a bit too much for what the situation warrants. When* **Manda** *comes to the kitchen doorstep and takes a flamboyant drag on her cigarette, they all watch, impressed.*

Simone All right Manda?

Manda All right, *kids?*

Kelly Does your mum let you smoke in the house?

Manda (*tuts*) Who listens to their mum?

Richard Let's have a bit.

Manda *stares at him. She takes a big drag and then blows the smoke in his direction.*

Manda Suck that in.

Simone We're drinkings spritzers, int we Kell?

Kelly Yeah they're gorgeous int they?

Simone Yeah.

Manda (*tuts*) I used to drink spritzers when I was about three.

Richard What d'you drink now then?

Manda G and T. On the rocks.

Kelly *looks over the fence to next door.*

Kelly Is that Gemma Sweeney up there?

Simone Where?

Kelly In that window.

Manda (*tuts*) Probably. She *is* our next door neighbour.

Simone What a monster.

Kelly Spotty bitch from hell.

Manda Well at least her spots are on her face Kell, and not on her arse. (*Goes indoors.*)

Richard She gets fitter every time I see her.

Simone You wanna get Gemma Sweeney to meet your mum Rich. Use her face for a new design for a pizza.

Kelly (*shouts up to window*) You stay where you are! This aint a dogs' party!

Simone (*holding clenched fist up to window*) Yeah or you'll get that!

Kelly Yeah! Dog!

Simone She's drawn her curtains!!

Richard Only thing she'll ever pull init?

They fall about laughing. **Viv** *and* **Joe** *come to the back door step.* **Tammy** *and* **David** *squeeze past them and out onto the patio.* **Joe** *and* **Viv** *are smoking.*

Viv Here kids, look what the cat dragged in!

Joe Hiya!

Kids All right Sir?

Viv Sir?! He's not your teacher tonight! Call him Joe. (*The kids laugh.*) He's here as a friend of the family's.

Richard All right, *Joe*? (*They laugh.*)

Joe Oh I mighta known you'd be here, Dicky. Okay Dick? (*Laughter.*)

Kelly Sir's got a fag, look!

Simone Oh no! And after all that work we done on it in PSE an' all Sir!

Viv Call him Joe or you'll be out on your arse!

Joe Are yous all enjoying the rave then?

Simone Yeah.

Kelly Richard's pissed, Sir.

Richard I can't help it, I'm a alcoholic.

David You aint old enough to be a alcoholic!

Simone You can't tell us off for swearing, right Sir, coz we're not in school now.

Joe Oh heaven help me. If my mother knew I mixed with the likes of you, she'd have me hung, drawn and quartered.

David I don't swear.

Kelly Boffin!

Simone Viv lets us swear, don't you Viv?

Viv Well I'm not your mother am I?

Tammy She lets me swear all the time.

Viv Only in me own four walls madam. I catch you swearing in school and you'll feel the back o'my hand. Be warned.

David I don't see the point of swearing.

Joe Nice one lad.

Viv Yeah well maybe when you're a bit bigger, eh Dave? Now Joe, tell me, what's your poison?

Joe Ooh a lager wouldn't go amiss Viv.

Viv Nice and frothy hey? I know your sort! (*Exits.*)

Joe Ooh yeah, shove that down me gullet, I'll be laughing!

Simone Sir drinks!

Kelly We've just had a drinking contest Sir. You know, like sports day, only with booze.

David That's stupid.

Richard I won it!

Joe That's coz you've got a big hole Rich.

Simone You can join in the next one if you like Sir.

David Sir's got more sense.

Tammy Call him Joe, that's his name!

Joe I hope none of yous lot's gonno have a hangover on Monday. If there's any absences I'll know why.

Simone Don't be daft, hangovers only last twenty-four hours.

Joe Well pardon me for being alcoholically ignorant.

Richard *attempts to go indoors, squeezing past* **Joe**.

Richard Scuse me, *Joe*! (**Kelly** *and* **Simone** *laugh,* **Richard** *exits.*)

Tammy What's so funny?

David Yeah!

Kelly Nothing. Sorry Sir.

Viv *comes to the door with a can of lager.*

Viv D'you wanna glass for this Joe?

Joe No you're all right.

Viv (*to the kids*) Right I want yous all inside and dancing. Go and keep my mother-in-law company, go on. You're here to party, so be told.

Simone, **Kelly**, **Tammy** *and* **David** *go indoors.*

David See you later Sir.

Viv Joe! (*Smacks* **David** *over the head as he goes in.*)

Joe See you.

Viv *and* **Joe** *are alone together. They stroll onto the patio.*

Joe Lovely night isn't it?

Viv Knockout. 'Ere look, full moon!

Joe Oh yeah!

Viv You know what they say about a full moon dunt ya?

Joe What's that?

Sonia *appears over the fence.*

Sonia My budgie's done toilets all down me curtains. That's three times this month I've had me nets in the Hotpoint.

Viv Oh Sonia no!

Sonia Mm. Here, I can't get me front door to open. Will you go out and give it a push Viv?

Viv Climb over the fence, it's quicker.

Sonia My back.

Viv Don't go away, I'll get the stepladder. (*Exits.*)

Sonia Hello.

Joe Hiya.

Sonia We got a chihuahua cross, three cats, two love-birds and a budgie in there. I think my husband was Noah in a past life. I don't like letting the budgie out, but he says it's only fair. You're Mr Casey, aren't you?

Joe That's right.

Sonia I've seen you before. At Parents' Evening. You had a little card on your desk, said 'Mr Casey'. I'm sorry, I can't remember your first name.

Joe Joe. Joe. As in Bloggs. Or Soap. Or Bugner.

Sonia I'm Sonia Sweeney. My daughter's Gemma Sweeney. She's in Mr Burgess' class, only she don't like him. He's a bit fierce, in'e? Comes over a bit strong sometimes, you know. I'm sure he doesn't mean to, only Gemma's got special needs, you know, and sometimes he forgets. Like say she's not filled in her homework diary, he throws a real tantrum, and see what he doesn't understand is, she can't write. I give her a form, made it up meself on a computer at work, it's like a special sheet. And she's supposed to ask the teachers to fill the homeworks in for her. On the form. Only she's afraid. Coz some of the teachers shout, or haven't got time. I mean I don't blame 'em, they've got enough on their plates with lairy kids and that, you know. So, I write endless letters to him, but he never writes back.

Joe I don't think PE teachers know how do they?

Sonia And see she's got a bad hip. Chronic. So she can't even do forward rolls, so he forgets who she is, coz come PE, she goes and helps Mrs Norman, in the library. She's nice that Mrs Norman, isn't she?

Joe Oh she's marvellous.

Sonia She was ever so nice over the business with the IST. Sorry, Individual Support Teacher. See, they took Gemma's off of her.

Joe Goway!

Sonia Mm. I had to go to an appeal. You know. And they're not the nicest of things, appeals. I come out in a big sweat and kept sliding off me seat. It didn't look good.

Joe Oh they're unspeakable those appeals aren't they?

Viv *guides* **Manda** *on.* **Manda** *is carrying a set of stepladders.* **Manda** *has a fag hanging out of her mouth. They make their way over to the fence.*

Sonia It's Gemma I feel sorry for.

Joe Ah, no luck?

Sonia It's the cuts init?

Joe God, tell me about it! We dunno who's for the chop next.

Viv (*to* **Manda**) Put it on the other side and Joe can lift her over.

Manda You wanna get a gate fitted on this fence Sonia.

Sonia My Brenda might get in and poo on your patio then.

Manda *lifts the ladders and arranges them over the fence.*

Viv Poo?! Nobody says poo any more Sonia.

Sonia Well I do.

Manda Stand back Sonia you're in the way.

Sonia Sorry.

Viv You got big muscles Joe? Up to a spot o'lifting?

Joe Do I look like one o'the Gladiators?

Viv Well I dunno. I'd have to see you in thigh-high lycra before I made me mind up. (*Squeezing his biceps.*) Mind you, you're quite brawny.

Sonia I could always pole vault over. (*She laughs at her own joke.*)

Viv Come on Joe, I'll give you an 'and. (*Winks.*)

Now the stepladders are set up on **Sonia**'s *side of the fence. She climbs up to the top.* **Joe**, **Viv** *and* **Manda** *crowd round ready to lift her down.*

Sonia (*climbing up slowly*) I'm afraid Ernie's stuck in Birmingham.

Manda Oh yes? Working late is he?

Viv Shut up Mand.

Sonia He had a big run on.

Viv You mean he aint gonna come?

Sonia His big end's gone. Who's lifting me?

Viv All hands on deck.

Joe Right then.

Viv And no touching her up Joe, she's a married woman!

Sonia Don't worry Joe, I've always had a strong regard for members of the teaching profession.

Manda If you mean teachers then why don't you just say it? (*Tuts.*)

Sonia *sits at the top of the stepladder with her legs hanging over the fence.*

Sonia Coz some of us have got breeding.

Viv Yeah Mand, that's something you don't know nothing about.

Manda I thank my lucky stars. I wouldn't wanna be like you.

Viv (*to* **Joe**) Are they all as bad as her?

Joe Worse.

Manda Cheeky bitch!

Sonia It's nice up here.

Viv Okay Son?

Sonia Think so.

They each hold onto a part of **Sonia**.

Viv One two three, lift!

They lift her down.

Viv Watch where you're putting them big hands o'yours Joe!

Sonia (*as they lift her*) Gemma's locked herself in her bedroom. (*They put her down.*) Thanks very much.

Viv Take them ladders back in now Mand. D'you know Sonia, Joe?

Manda (*getting the ladders*) What did your last slave die of?

Viv Ugliness.

Joe Yeah, we've met.

Viv Sonia's my next-door-neighbour.

Manda (*exiting with ladders*) Oh you don't say!

Viv (*tuts*) D'you know Sonia's daughter? Gemma? She's got really bad skin. But she's quite pretty underneath it aint she Sonia?

Sonia Well we can't all be perfect can we?

Viv No we can't. Now Sonia, what's your poison? Cinzano and ice?

Sonia Oh fresh orange Viv, it's my back.

Viv You boring old fart! Freeze and a squeeze?

Sonia What?

Viv Ice and Lemon. (*Winks at* **Joe**.)

Sonia Oh why not? Live a little, I say.

Viv You do that Son. (*Exiting.*) Coming right up, as the actress said to the bishop!

Viv *exits, laughing.*

Sonia (*stretching down, as if to pick up an imaginary object*) If I do that, it really hurts.

Joe I bet that's painful.

Sonia I was on a bus yesterday, and I had to get up and lie in the aisle.

Joe Oh you wanna get that seen to.

Sonia And it was the 380, you know those little buses, so there wasn't much room. I don't like those little buses, do you?

Joe Well er, can't say I'm a big fan, no.

Sonia So . . . how d'you find teaching in this neck of the woods? Is it pretty dicey?

Joe Well it's a bit of a challenge like, you know. Dodging the flying bricks, the petrol bombs. I'm getting used to the riot shield but the helmet brings me out in a terrible rash.

Sonia It must help, you coming from Liverpool. Coz that's pretty rough init? And I mean, some of the people round here have just given up. Myself and Vivian excluded. Never miss a Parents' Evening, and we go to all the concerts. My Gemma plays the tuba. She played 'Au Claire de la Lune' at the last concert. Did you hear her?

Joe No. I had a touch o'tonsilitis, but I heard she was very good.

Sonia Well did you go the Christmas Fair? Coz it was my husband what ran the 'Guess the Name o'the Donkey' stall. He got it off a mate of his who has a sanctuary up Erith way.

Joe Oh right I remember. (*Sniggers.*)

Sonia It was a nice donkey, Sophie, they called it. My husband wanted to keep it, but between you and me, my husband aint all there. (*Pause.*) Are you an employee of the Greenwich Council?

Joe For me sins.

Sonia Oh well, you and me both then.

Joe Really?

Sonia I work in a day-care centre up in Woolwich. With old people.

David *comes out and sits on the step with a plate of crisps.*

Joe Oh that's interesting.

Sonia Mm. I'm the secretary. I had untold interviews to get the job. They're an equal opportunities employer, the Greenwich Council, so it wasn't easy . . . me being white and all.

Viv (*off*) Tell him what they asked you!

Sonia They said to me, they said, you know, 'How would you feel, like, if you found you were working in an office with a known gay man.' D'you know what I mean?

Joe Goway!

Sonia I mean I knew it was only put there to fox me, coz I'd been in the office, and it was all women.

Joe Well what did you say?

Sonia Told 'em the truth. Speak as you find, I say.

Viv *comes out with a glass of orange for* **Sonia**.

Viv Okay Dave?

David Yeah, I'm really enjoying myself.

Viv Sonia?

Sonia (*taking glass*) Thanks. Do you believe in reincarnation Mr Casey?

Joe What, Buddhism and all that?

Sonia No, reincarnation. Only I do, right, and let me tell you this, I firmly believe that once upon a time, gay men were women in a past life. D'you know what I mean? And like, now, in their present life, the femininity in them . . . is coming out. To coin a phrase. D'you follow me?

Viv Interesting init?

Joe Yeah. And is that what you said?

Sonia Yeah, well I know a lot about reincarnation. I'm a member of the Erith Nine Lives Association, and we all sit around and connect with our former selves. You call it deja vu. I call it connection. Yeah? I mean if you was to come into my house you'd get quite a shock, coz I firmly believe that once upon a time I lived in a country cottage. And so my house is full of country cottagey type things. It's got a really cottagey feel to it. You know, little cottages made out of stone, a copper kettle over the fireplace, that sort o'thing. And when we go to the country, my husband's a coach driver, so sometimes I sit up front with him. Well sometimes, when we go to the country, I feel really at home. I don't wanna come back. Do I Viv?

Viv Tell him about the woman with the blonde hair Sonia. Listen to this Joe.

Sonia I think I was murdered once. By a woman with a peroxide beehive and a shopping trolley. Well I'm pretty sure of it actually.

Viv She gets flashbacks, don't you Son?

Sonia I do.

Joe God.

Sonia We're in a marketplace. It's a Saturday, mid afternoon. She's holding my hand and I don't want to go. It's busy. There's loads of people about. She talks all northern. 'Come little girl, come.'

Viv Well you know who it is Joe?

Joe No?

Sonia ⎫
Viv ⎭ Myra Hindley!!

Sonia You won't tell anyone, will you?

Joe No.

Viv No, don't tell anyone Joe. She might get a reputation for being a loony.

Sonia This is it, init?

Joe But wouldn't you have been alive when Myra Hindley was . . . you know.

Sonia The spirit world moves in mysterious ways I say. I've read 'Devil's Disciples', 'Beyond Belief' and I'm halfway through 'Myra: Inside the Mind of a Murderess' so I'm pretty convinced as it goes.

Viv Know any journalists JoJo?

Joe No I don't.

Viv Oh, shame that. Coz it's a big story init?

Joe Suppose so.

Sonia Is Kenny here yet Viv?

Viv Been and gone, but coming back for more. Just the way I like them.

Sonia Have you met Viv's brother yet?

Joe No.

Sonia Oh he's lovely Kenny, it's a shame.

Joe Oh?

Viv Sonia!

Sonia Sorry.

Joe What?

Sonia Nothing.

Viv David? Go and dance love. Tammy'll be wondering where you've got to.

David I'm all right here.

Viv This is grown-ups talk Dave so shufty please.

David (*gets up*) Sorry. (*Exits.*)

Sonia I'm saying nothing.

Viv See thing is Joe . . . my brother, Kenny . . .

Sonia D'you ever do crosswords Joe?

Joe I have a crack at the *Guardian* now and again.

Sonia Right. Well say we was doing a crossword, yeah, and the word we was looking for was Kenny. The clue would be . . . three letter word rhyming with Fay. Or Fomosexual. Yep?

Viv Comprendez, Joe Boy?

Joe And this is Kenny?

Viv Certainly is.

Joe Oh right.

Viv I love him. Don't get me wrong, but I always feel I gotta warn people before they meet him. Fairer both sides then init?

Sonia Did you get the clue Joe? He's gay.

Viv I mean he aint a pouf or nothing. He's been a boxer, a soldier, he's done modelling . . .

Sonia Catalogue modelling . . .

Viv Yeah. Freemans. He aint . . .

Sonia Effeminatey.

Viv No, he aint what you could call effeminatey. You ask Lulu. She was nuts about him when he did the Freemans catalogue.

Sonia Said he was all man.

Viv All man.

Sonia But some people are prejudiced, int they?

Joe They are.

Viv Just in case . . .

Joe What?

Sonia He tries anything.

Viv I mean he probably won't.

Sonia No he probably won't.

Viv No.

Sonia But you never know, do you?

Viv This is the nature of the beast. Mm?

Sonia Would that offend you?

Joe Oh no. Not at all.

Viv Blinding. Coz I love him Joe, d'you know what I mean? He's me own flesh and blood, and I'd hate to see him shunned.

Sonia I told you Viv. I said didn't I?

Viv She did.

Sonia The London Borough of Greenwich is an equal opportunities employer. Joe must have gay men and lesbian women coming out of his ears in his line of business.

Viv I can always tell him to steer well clear Joe . . .

Joe Oh there's no need really. Sonia's right, you'd be surprised at like, the amount of gay people I've actually met. You know.

Viv Oh blinding. Coz I'd like you to meet him. I'd like you to meet all the family. And me and him's like that. (*Holds two fingers up, intertwined.*) Coz he's lovely, inn'e Son?

Sonia Well he's gentle. In a . . . rough . . . sort o'way.

Viv You've summed him up there Sonia.

Sonia (*sniffs*) Well when you've had as many lives as I have, you know your dictionary inside out.

Joe Fab.

Sonia (*sniffs*) I do apologise. (*Looks at her shoe.*) I've stepped in one of my Brenda's little presents.

Viv I wondered what the smell was. Thought it was Joe letting off. I know you vegetarians, it's all beans and roughage init? Very gassy.

Sonia I better wash it off.

Viv Come on Son I'll get you a cloth.

Sonia Oh you're too kind.

Viv No I'll just rip up one of Scottie's old shirts. (*To* **Joe**.) Are you, er, coming in sweetheart?

Joe As the actress said to the bishop. (*Giggles.*)

Viv (*to* **Sonia**) Ooh in 'e saucy eh? I like a man with sauce dun'I Son?

Sonia I wouldn't know.

Viv You see a man to me is like a plate of chips. And a plate of chips aint a plate of chips without a bit o'sauce!

Joe *mounts the step.* **Viv** *smacks him playfully on the bum.*

Joe Ooh! Watch me hoop!

Viv I'm watching I'm watching! (*Laughs.*)

Joe *wiggles his bum and goes in.* **Sonia** *smacks* **Viv** *on the bum as she goes in.*

Sonia So am I.

They go in.

Manda *comes out shortly with a fag and a can of lager. She stares into the audience. Then she reaches her hand inside the kitchen door and* *pulls out a telephone on a long cable – a wall phone. She dials a number, still staring into the audience. She is ringing her boyfriend who lives in the flats at the back of her house.*

Manda (*into phone*) Siddie? Siddie? . . . (*Tuts.*) Go and stand by your window . . . (*She waves.*) Wave back . . . (*Smiles.*) Meet me down the Sewage in ten minutes, I got something for you . . . Well that's for me to know and you to find out init?

Richard *and* **Kelly** *run out having a peanut fight. They scream as they throw peanuts at each other, darting to and fro on the patio.*

Manda Shut up! Yous two shut up! Can't you see I'm making a call? (*To phone.*) Siddie?

Richard *and* **Kelly** *calm down and try to fight in silence. They giggle.*

Manda (*into phone, tuts*) What? . . . Who's that at the window with you? Siddie? . . . Is that Pastel Pinkney? . . . oh Siddie . . . oh fuck you then!

She puts the phone back indoors. She sticks two fingers up at the audience.

Ernie *pops his head over the fence.* **Ernie** *is* **Sonia***'s husband. He is early-forties and wears Farah slacks, with fly down, a sports shirt and Hush Puppies.*

Ernie Manda! Psst! Manda!

Manda (*tuts*) I thought you was in Birmingham.

Ernie Come over here.

Manda Why?

Ernie Come and have a butchers at this!

Manda (*walking over*) Your wife said your big end was giving you jip.

Ernie Hurry up!

He holds a sack over the fence, and opens it so **Manda** *can have a look inside.* **Kelly** *and* **Richard** *share a can of lager.*

Manda Aw Ernie! Let's have it!

Ernie It's a present for the old girl init?

Manda Shall I go and tell her?

Ernie What d'you reckon she's gonna say?

Manda I dunno. I'm not psychic am I?

Ernie Go and get her, but don't let on.

Manda All right, all right, keep your hair on. What's left of it. (*Goes in.*)

Ernie Here, fatty!

Kelly What?

Ernie And you. Hold this while I jumps over.

Richard What?

Ernie Don't drop it, whatever you do.

He hands them the sack. **Kelly** *looks in.*

Kelly Aw, init cute?!

Richard (*into bag*) Boo! (*Laughs.*)

Kelly Don't, you'll wake it up!

Ernie *jumps the fence, and goes flying, falling flat on his face.* **Kelly** *and* **Richard** *have a real laugh about this.*

Ernie Fuckinell! (*Struggles to get up.*) Don't help me will you?

Sonia *comes to the step, wiping one of her shoes with a cloth. She walks a few paces onto the patio. The rest of the cast, bar* **Ivy**, *follow her out gawping.*

Sonia What happened to Birmingham?

Ernie Oh all right love?

Sonia I hope you didn't jump that fence Ernie. You were not, and I stress, were not Olga Korbut in a past life, and never will be!

Kelly (*to everyone else*) Look at this!

Sonia I thought you was . . . Oh don't tell me, Birmingham's gonna be Welwyn Garden City all over again.

Ernie Well it's a surprise, init?

Everyone else crowds around the sack. 'Coos' and 'ahs' from all concerned.

Sonia Your daughter's locked herself in her bedroom. Think she was Rapunzel in another life.

Ernie I got you something there.

Sonia Are you receiving me? Son to Ern. Delta Tango Foxtrot. I said Gemma's locked herself in her room!

Ernie (*to* **Kelly**, *taking the sack*) Give us that.

Simone What's its name?

Ernie Cut it out! Have a look in here Sonia love.

Sonia Why do I get the feeling I'm not gonna like this?

Viv Coz you were a chromosome away from being Doris Stokes, Son. Have a look go on.

Sonia Confirm my worst fears.

Ernie Come on babe.

Ernie *holds the sack open.* **Sonia** *peers in. A look of annoyance covers her face.*

Ernie This bird up Birmingham found it at the side of the motorway. Abandoned it was.

Sonia Vivian? Get me that Cinzano.

Manda I'll have it if you don't want it Sonia.

Viv (*exiting*) No you won't Madam.

Ernie It was gonna get put down babe. Look at its face.

Sonia It's rabid.

Ernie Don't say that, it might hear.

Sonia What sort is it?

Ernie Alsatian.

Sonia No Ernie. You know I don't like big dogs.

Ernie It's only a puppy.

Sonia You say that now.

Tammy Can we have it?

Kelly I saw it first!

Manda I fucking did!

Tammy Yeah and it's my birthday!

Ernie This dog's mine! Yous can all stop gawping and piss off inside!

Sonia Ernie!

Ernie Go on!

They all filter back in.

Sonia One of them was a teacher Ern.

Ernie Teachers. Fucking nosiest of the lot.

Sonia Why d'you have to be so moany with kids?

Ernie Oh look, me fly's undone.

Sonia No thank you.

Viv *comes in with a Cinzano.*

Viv Sonia? Get this down you.

Sonia Cheers. I couldn't have an Alsatian Ern. I wouldn't feel in control.

Ernie You would be.

Sonia As soon as you'd go out, it'd turn on me.

Ernie Just shout at it!

Sonia You'll have to get rid of it.

Ernie I saved this mutt from a fate worse than death.

Sonia Nothing wrong with death Ernie. We all come back.

Ernie Oh we'll stick it in the oven and gas it shall we? Come on.

Sonia What would it do Ern? I'll tell you what, it'd chew me furniture and have my little Brenda for afters. She'd be a soft toy within a week.

Ernie I'll take it down the pub then. Someone there's bound to have a bit of feeling in 'em.

Sonia You could try prising your daughter out of her room first.

Ernie Let her stew. I'm going 'The Wildfowler'.

Viv Get us a large bottle o'tonic while you're down there Ern. We're running low.

Ernie If you want.

Sonia I dread every job you do. Dunno what you'll bring back. Snakes and everything I wouldn't wonder.

Ernie I'm an animalist. Can't help that.

Sonia They eat dogs in China.

Enter **Joe** *with an unlit cigarette.*

Joe Got a light Viv?

Viv There you go. (*Passes her fag for him to get a light off it.*) Ern, this is Joe.

Ernie Right?

Viv Tammy's teacher, and a very close personal friend.

Ernie Fuck me, are you a teacher?

Joe Yeah.

Ernie Cor he don't look old enough does he?

Joe I'm twenty-four.

Viv That's a lovely age.

Ernie You don't want a dog do you?

Joe Er . . . no . . . not really.

Ernie Alsatian, fifty quid. But seeing as how you're Tammy's teacher, you can have it for forty.

Sonia Ernie!

Ernie It's a good offer.

Joe No I've only got a small flat.

Viv Live on your own Joe?

Joe No. I share.

Viv What, with a girlfriend or something?

Joe No. Just a friend.

Viv Friendship's a wonderful thing.

Ernie Alsatians make good guard dogs you know.

Sonia That's what he said about my chihuahua. Ern, he doesn't want it.

Ernie Give the man a chance Sonia.

Joe I'm sorry.

Sonia You don't have to apologise to him, he's soft.

Ernie Jees . . . I rescues a little life, and bring it to a good home, where he could have . . . have love, and big long walks . . . instead of getting electrocuted bars shoved through his head . . .

Sonia Got a violin Mr Casey? Play it.

Ernie (*looking in sack*) It's crying Sonia. It's got tears running down its face. I had to Sonia.

Sonia You'll have to excuse my husband Mr Casey, he's had a hard life.

Ernie Not as hard as this poor mutt.

Sonia He was brought up on a barge.

Viv (*to* **Joe**) Tell us a bit about Liverpool. I love the Liverpoolian accent.

Ernie It's shaking Sonia.

Sonia I'll shake you in a minute.

Viv It's probably that Barry Grant off *Brookside*, but I just have to hear a Scouse accent and I go all . . .

Sonia I think he was Tarzan in another life.

Viv Moist. Ah! Weak at the knees.

Ernie If I was Tarzan now, I wouldn't swing through the jungle for you.

Sonia You'd slip off your rope.

Viv D'you watch *Brookside*?

Sonia You'd be wallowing around in swamp.

Joe No, it's not that reflective of how Liverpool is really.

Viv Really? You know, I didn't know that.

Ernie (*to* **Joe**) Hold still, you got a wasp on you.

Joe Have I?

Ernie Don't move.

Sonia Oh flick it off.

Ernie Cut it out Sonia.

Sonia Go on, flick it off before it stings him.

Ernie Are you crazy?

Sonia No!

Ernie How would you like it if a whalloping great big . . .

Viv I'll do it. (*Flicks* **Joe***'s shoulder.*) Sorry Joe, did I hurt you?

Joe No.

Ernie I don't believe you did that Viv!

Viv (*to* **Joe**) Let me give it a rub.

Joe Er . . .

Viv I didn't mean to hurt you Joe.

Ernie (*making his way out*) I'm surrounded by murderers! (*To* **Sonia**.) I'll be back closing time.

Sonia If you're gonna be like that Ernie, I don't want you coming back.

Ernie Fair enough. (*Exits.*)

Sonia I'm sorry Viv. Really.

Viv (*to* **Joe**, *still rubbing*) You're quite broad shouldered, in a deceptive way.

Joe Am I?

Viv Oh God yeah.

Sonia I think it's on account of him our Gem has special needs.

Viv I got special needs. In the underwear department.

Sonia I think you should have a big black coffee dear.

Viv I wondered what you was gonna say then!

Joe I'll have to go the loo.

Sonia Top of the stairs. It's got 'Yere Tiz' written on the door.

Joe Oh God, call the kitsch police!

Viv What?

Joe Nothing.

Sonia No it's not in the kitchen. Top of the stairs.

Viv Next to my bedroom. No peeking now, d'you hear?

Joe I'll try me best. (*Exits.*)

Viv I can tell him where me own bloody toilet is thank you Sonia!

Sonia You wanna go easy on the drink Viv, d'you hear?

Viv I'm a free agent in'I?

Sonia Think of Scottie, I say.

Viv Oh you're turning into a right little Valerie Pinkney you are! You've got a problem with enjoying yourself you have.

Sonia Scottie died on this patio! I can feel his presence all around me.

Viv Oh Sonia, do you have to?

Sonia He's touching me Viv!

Viv Well don't hold your breath, he was useless at foreplay.

Sonia No Viv, he's communicating with me.

Viv Well if it's a smack in the teeth Sonia, don't say I didn't warn ya!

Sonia You shouldn't say things like that Viv.

Viv Why not? It's the truth init?

Sonia He's listening.

Viv That makes a change.

Sonia He's saying . . .

Viv What?

Sonia He's telling you . . .

Viv No. No Son. I had sixteen years of being told what to do. He's dead Sonia, Scottie's dead. I'm alive. And I wanna enjoy myself. I'm a single woman. Now get in there and get boogieing.

Sonia Yeah well if it's all the same with you Vivian I'm gonna slip next door and see if I can't get my Gemma out of her bedroom. I got an husband tryina convert me home into London Zoo, a daughter in the depths of puberty, and bad back. So actually no Vivian, I don't think I will get boogieing actually.

Viv Oh be like that.

Sonia Yeah I will.

Viv *makes to go indoors, and* **Sonia** *makes to follow. They are about to go in when all the kids come out of the house in a human chain,* *doing the conga.* **Sonia** *and* **Viv** *stand and watch.* **Manda** *and* **Richard** *are at the front, followed by* **Simone**, **Kelly**, **Tammy** *and* **David**. **Sonia** *goes indoors as the conga circles the patio.*

Manda Back in the house!

Richard What?!

Manda Back in the house!

Richard All right!

Manda *swings round, changing the direction of the conga. She heads for the back door and exits. The line follows suit.* **Viv** *brings up the rear, but stops short of exiting and looks up into the sky.*

Viv Yeah Valerie Pinkney! I'm having a good time! I'm loving it! I'll have you Valerie Pinkney! Just you wait and see! I'll fucking have you Valerie Pinkney! Just you see if I don't!

Viv *goes to exit, but it's as though the sky is saying something to her.*

Viv Yeah! Go on! Try it!

Viv *exits.*

Act Two

Scene One

Sonia's *landing*

As before, **Sonia** *stands outside* **Gemma**'s *bedroom door. This time she sings to her.*

Sonia (*sings*) Mister Bear? Are you there?
    Don't you dare to take a bite of me.
    If you do I'll scream and quick
    My ole man'll fetch his stick
    Coz he aint afraid o'bears, not he.
    So if you want a little baby girl
    And you're hungry
    And you can't wait any more,
    I can tell you where there's plenty
    Have a try at number twenty.
    Yes go and bite the little girl next door
    Go and bite the little girl next door.
    (*Soft chuckle.*)
D'you like that Gem? Sang that in nursery I did. (*Pause.*)
You coming the party Gem? You can drink you know. Oh
it's a really lovely party. Real . . . lovely. (*Pause.*) Bathroom's
a bit of a mess Gem. And I did spy with my little eye an
empty bottle of Born Blonde. You . . . experimenting . . .
Gem? I know you got my curling tongs, coz they aint on my
tall boy. Do your hair Gem, doll yourself up. That's the
spirit. We'll all be waiting for you.

She walks off.

Scene Two

Viv's bedroom

As before, double bed, dressing table stool. **Tammy** *and* **David** *sit on the bed.* **Tammy** *has her arm round him awkwardly. He drinks a can of coke. She drinks a glass of what looks like coke.*

Tammy If you had a million pounds, what would you do?

David Give it poor people, how 'bout you?

Tammy I'd give me mum a bit, and me Uncle Kenny a bit. I'd give some to Gemma for facelift, and I'd spend the rest on clothes and world peace.

David Would you?

Tammy Yeah.

David If you had a button, and you had to press that button, and like, a million people would die in Australia or somewhere dead far away . . . would you press it?

Tammy No.

David No. I wouldn't. Richard would.

Tammy Richard's a prat.

David Are you ever gonna smoke?

Tammy Dunno. Might do. In moderation.

David Are you ever gonna drink?

Tammy I'm drinking now!

David Are you?

Tammy Yeah. Only in moderation though.

David What's moderation mean?

Tammy Not much.

David It must mean something.

Tammy No that's what it means, not much.

David Are you gonna have sex before you're sixteen?

Tammy Dunno.

David I'm not.

Tammy No?

David No. Unless I'm in a caring relationship with a bird. And even then, I'll only do it in moderation.

Tammy Oh.

David D'you miss your dad?

Tammy Yeah.

David Did he go all baldy?

Tammy A bit. He was cremated.

David Ah.

Tammy Me mum's got him under the bed, in a pot.

David This bed?!

Tammy She's waiting to take him up Allhallows-on-Sea. That's where they met. They were teenage runaways. But she aint had the time off work yet.

David Right.

Tammy D'you wanna see him?

David Nah. Nah, you're all right. Maybe some other time. Yeah?

Tammy All right.

Kenny *enters.*

Tammy Uncle Kenny!

Kenny All right Tammy? Someone in the bog?

David Sir is.

Tammy Joe is.

Toilet flushes. Off.

Kenny Oh Joe, I've heard a lot about him.

Tammy Joe! Joe!

Joe *pops his head round the door.*

Joe Hiya!

Kenny All right? You Joe then?

Joe Kenny?

Kenny Well if I'm not, me Calvin Kleins are a good fit, d'you know what I mean?!

David (*to* **Tammy**) He's funny in'e?

Tammy (*to* **David**) He's my uncle.

Kenny Down on your own Joe?

Joe (*to* **Kenny**) Fraid so.

Kenny Oh well, we'll have to make sure you don't go lonely. Wait up, I gotta go toilet.

Joe Oh sorry. (*Steps out of* **Kenny**'s *way.*)

Kenny Don't apologise to me, unless you've pissed on the seat. Viv'll get the right hump! (*Laughs as he exits.*)

David You had anything to eat yet Sir? Sorry. I find it hard calling you Joe.

Joe That's okay David.

David There's cheese sandwiches and crisps and cake for vegetarians, so you should be all right.

Joe Sounds good enough to eat.

Tammy Mum's dancing, Joe.

Joe Yeah?

Tammy Have a nice time, won't you Joe!

Joe Okay. I will. (*Exits.*)

David He doesn't fancy your mum does he?

Tammy You saying my mum's ugly or something?

David But he's twenty-four.

Tammy You calling my mum an ole slapper or something?

David He can't go with your mum Tammy.

Tammy Says who?

David He's our teacher!

Tammy But my dad's dead. If they get together . . .

David But Joe lives up Charlton, it's miles away!

Tammy It's only on the fucking 180 bus!

David Don't start swearing Tammy, it aint nice!

Tammy Bloody hell. I'd think you was a boffin if you was brainy!

David I don't like birds who swear!

Tammy I want him to be my new stepdad! I want Joe to be my new dad!

David No!

Tammy Yeah!

David Oh bloody hell Tammy, you gotta put a stop to it before it gets out of hand!

Tammy Oh go and play with your oboe!

Manda *suddenly enters.*

Manda Oi! Who gave you permission to come in here?!

Tammy Oh get lost Manda this is a personal conversation . . .

Manda Out of here now! You know mum don't allow it!

David I'm sorry Manda.

Tammy Don't apologise to her!

Manda Get yourself and your piss ugly boyfriend out of here before I slap the face of you!

Tammy Take that back what you said about my bloke!

David It don't matter Tam!

Tammy (*to* **David**) I'm sticking up for you here!

Manda D'you want me to get mum? Do you?

Tammy We weren't doing nothing!

David I never laid a finger on her!

Manda Oh yeah?

Tammy He hasn't got it in him!

Enter **Kenny**.

Kenny Oi! What's all the bloody noise?

Manda Oh Kenny. Mum said bedrooms was out of bounds. I caught them two at it on me own mother's bed!

Tammy Bollocks!

Kenny Come on yous two, if that's what Viv's said.

David I'm really sorry about this Mr Williams, but it aint the way it seems . . .

Tammy I wouldn't let him near me!

Manda (*to* **David**, *as* **Tammy** *exits*) And don't think you're coming to my party when I'm having one!

David I'd rather stick pins in me eyes! (*Exits.*)

Manda Oi!!

Kenny Manda!

Manda What?!

Kenny Calm down woman.

Manda *gets a fag out and lights up. She is left with* **Kenny**.

Kenny Who rattled your cage, you miserable bitch?

Manda's *not saying*.

Manda (*tuts*) Shut up.

Kenny Who?

Manda (*tuts*) No one. Get outa my face Kenny all right?

Kenny Manda.

Manda Take three guesses. It begins with S and ends in E.

Kenny What did I say?

Manda Oh don't you start.

Kenny What's he done now?

Manda What hasn't he done? I've chucked him anyway.

Kenny Come here you.

They sit on the bed and hug.

Kenny Don't upset yourself.

Manda He's such a bastard.

Kenny He aint worth it. Come on. Plenty more frogs in the pond.

Manda Why's he like that Kenny?

Kenny Law of the jungle babes. That's the way blokes are.

Manda What, like little shits?

Kenny One day, you'll meet a nice bloke. You'll be walking down the street. And he'll catch your eye. And he'll give you the look. And you'll just know he's mad about you. And he'll . . . he'll just be the most gorgeous bloke in the world. A nice bloke . . .

Manda Like you?

Kenny Yeah.

Manda Well he'll be gay then won't he?

Kenny There are some blokes left who aren't. God knows where, but there are.

Manda Kenny?

Kenny Babe?

Manda Is this how you felt after that Reebok-Step-Class Instructor?

Kenny Well . . . that was a little bit different babe . . . he was a waster. Wasters aint worth it. You gotta set your aims high. Little Mister Reebok was goin nowhere.

Manda Yeah. I never liked him.

Kenny I never liked Siddie. Looks like we both need a new bloke.

Manda Yeah. We'll have to find you someone Kenny.

Kenny Find me that teacher then.

Manda You like Joe?!

Kenny I'm aiming high.

Manda He's not one of yours.

Kenny Excuse me but you're speaking to a man with GCSE Queenspotting.

Manda Mum wants to get his knickers off.

Kenny She's not the only one. Anything down there you fancy?

Manda That Richard won't leave me alone. But he's just a kid. I can aim higher than that.

Kenny Ah but once in a while a girl needs spoiling. Come on. Let's get some dutch courage and get ourselves spoilt.

They giggle, get up and leave the room.

Scene Three

Viv's lounge

A loud blast of conga music. Immediately the last scene finishes, a conga procession enters the lounge. **Kenny** *and* **Manda** *gradually join it, with* **Manda** *pushing in and getting behind* **Richard**. *At the front* **Viv** *is pushing* **Ivy** *in her chair. Everyone else is behind. Bringing up the rear is* **Joe**, *closely followed, and snugly held, by* **Kenny**. *Everyone is having a good time.*

Viv Kick your legs Ive, go on!

The conga circles the room. **Viv** *drops out of the line and* **Sonia** *takes over the controls of* **Ivy**'s *chair. She swivels the line round and they start to head for the door.* **Viv** *stands in the middle of the room, conducting them with her outstretched arms. She notices the closeness of*

Kenny *to* **Joe** *at the back, and as the line disappears into the hall she grabs* **Kenny** *and shuts the door.*

Viv What d'you think you're playing at, you ole tart?!

Kenny Same game as you probably!

Viv Yeah well hands off, I seen him first.

Kenny Vivian, the lad's queer.

Viv Oh he is, is he?

Kenny Can't you see it?

Viv No Kenny, and shall I tell you why? Because he's fucking straight! You think you know everything don't you? Well you don't, do you? Every bloke you meet is gay, according to you. Guilty 'til proven innocent, with you.

Kenny And I'm always right, in'I?

Viv Well not this time you aint. Not by a long shot.

Kenny Vivian . . .

Viv No Kenny. Don't wreck my night. He's here in good faith and I don't want him upsetting. Our Tammy idolises that bloke and I don't want him thinking he's stepped into Sodom and Gerfuckinmorrah.

The door opens. **Manda** *stands in the doorway, fingering a drink with a straw.*

Manda Yous two having a row?

Viv Leave it out Manda!

Manda D'you know what I reckon?

Viv Get in the kitchen now!

Manda I reckon he's bilingual.

Viv You! Move it!

Manda (*going*) Touchy touchy! (*Exits.*)

Viv I'll touch you in a minute!

Kenny (*closing the door*) Viv, if you must know . . .

Viv You take the piss once too often you do.

Kenny I've seen him in the pub.

Viv No. You're lying now.

Kenny With a blond lad!

The door opens. **Kelly** *and* **Simone** *come through.* **Richard** *follows shortly, pushing* **Ivy** *in the wheelchair.*

Viv What do you want?

Kelly Get somin to eat.

Simone Blindin' party Viv.

Viv Mrs Williams to you now hurry up!

They hurry up.

Richard Oright Mrs Williams?

Viv Shut up and get a drink. And mind her she's had three strokes!

Kenny Okay Ivy?

Simone, Kelly *and* **Richard** *exit with* **Ivy**, *leaving the door open.*

Viv (*shouting to them as she shuts the door*) Was you born in a stable?! (*To* **Kenny**.) What would a respectable teacher be doing in your fruity pub, hey? You talking through your arse.

Kenny We're not all hairdressers and trolley dollies, dear!

Viv You wanna spoil Tammy's night? Yeah? Well you know what you can do, don't you? (*To* **Kenny**, *as the door opens and* **Joe** *enters.*) You can get out now!

Joe *stands in the doorway and immediately backs away.*

Joe Oh what am I like? I'm the two ends o'Niagara Falls. I've gotta go the loo again. I'm like a tap me, turn it on, turn it off.

Kenny You got a weak bladder, never out that bloody bog!

Viv Shut up! Oright Joe?

Joe Bit pissed really.

Viv Aw, bless!

Joe Toilet. Or as they say on the Continent, dooble-vay-say. Ciao!

Joe *exits.*

Kenny I just don't wanna see you make a fool of yourself.

Viv You're in league with Valerie Pinkney you are. Tryina make me feel guilty, well it won't work.

Kenny Oh you're doing me head in now Viv.

Viv You and me both baby!

Kenny Oh forget I ever said anything.

Sonia *enters as* **Kenny** *attempts to leave. She closes the door behind her, blocking his way, and goes over to the food and starts picking, totally oblivious to* **Kenny** *and* **Viv**'s *row.*

Sonia Isn't that teacher a lovely man?

Viv (*to* **Kenny**) Oi! You can't get away with it that easy.

Kenny Spare me the lecture Viv. As per usual, you're lecturing to me about things you know fuck all about.

Sonia We've been having a chat and it looks like, it just . . . looks like . . . he was Bonnie Prince Charlie in a past life.

Viv (*to* **Kenny**) Watch me. I'm gonna ask him. Sort this out once and for all. Watch this.

Viv *flounces out of the room, leaving the door open behind her.* **Kenny** *shouts through.*

Kenny Oh for Gawd's sake! Viv!

Straight into Scene Four.

Scene Four

Viv's bedroom

Viv *stands in her room, bouffing her hair up. The toilet flushes off. She goes to the door.*

Viv Joe! Get in here!

Joe *entering, sings along to the song playing downstairs. Dancing.*

Viv Sit on the bed Joe.

Joe What?

Viv Just . . . sit on the bed. You all right?

Joe I'm pissed. I've hardly eaten anything.

Viv Can I ask you something? You won't take offence?

Joe Oh Viv I'm off me face.

Viv You see . . .

Joe It's nothing to do with school is it? If I've sent horrible letters home about homework it's only coz o'me Head of Department, she's a real bitch Viv, she doesn't understand me . . .

She joins him on the bed.

Viv Joe . . .

Joe She hates me.

Viv Joe . . .

Joe Mm?

Viv I know I'm being totally out of order here, but Joe, what bus are you on?

Joe Mm?

Viv The queenie bus? Or the straightie bus?

Joe What?

Viv You're not are you? (*Pause.*) Are you queenie? Or not queenie?

Joe Viv . . .

Viv Are you gay or straight?

Joe Oh don't do this to me Viv.

Viv Coz if you're straight, I'll have you, and if you're gay, Kenny'll have you.

Joe Oh ground open and swallow me up.

Viv Are you gay?

Pause.

Joe I'm sorry Viv. Really.

Viv Yeah?

Joe *reluctantly nods his head.*

Viv Jesus. Fucking queers! You're everywhere int you?

Joe Taking over the world Viv.

Viv I coulda sworn you was on my bus.

Joe It's difficult, you know, the kids and all that.

Viv Tell me about it. One whiff o'Kenny being a queer round here and . . . we'd be mincemeat.

Joe I know the feeling love.

Viv Ooh you can call me love any time dear. Here, your secret's safe with me you ole tart. Stay there. (*Gets up.*) Break our Tammy's heart if she knew. I couldn't do that to her.

Viv *exits. As she disappears we hear her calling to* **Kenny**.

Viv (*off*) He's all yours!!

Joe *takes a deep breath, then exhales a big sigh. He rests his head in his hands, still on the bed. Just then the door swings slowly open and* **Kenny** *enters.*

Pause, while **Kenny** *stands staring at* **Joe**.

Kenny Bit of a turn up for the books init.

Joe Christ, you don't waste any time do you?

Kenny Bet you're a big boy int ya?

Joe What?

Kenny (*winks*) Chop me off at the knees and call me tripod.

Joe No. No me dick's tiny. It's like a betting shop biro it's that small.

Kenny *goes over to him and sits on the bed and puts his hand on* **Joe***'s knee. He squeezes it.*

Kenny D'you work out?

Joe No.

Kenny *keeps his hand there, then runs it up and down.* **Joe** *doesn't respond.*

Kenny Just an old fashioned girl eh?

Joe Something like that.

Kenny Bollocks.

Joe I'm a bit pissed.

Pause.

Kenny You courting?

Joe I live with someone.

Kenny Are you faithful?

Joe So far.

Kenny I took one look at you and knew.

Joe Yeah? Well you've had years of practice haven't you?

Kenny Can I see ya?

Joe Where?

Kenny 'The Clutch and Handbag'.

Joe I dunno.

Kenny I can get you in for nothing.

Joe It's . . .

Kenny Embarrassed?

Joe No.

Kenny Good.

Pause.

D'you love him? (*Pause.*) What's he up to tonight then?
(*Beat.*) Out boozin'? (*Pause.*) Pretend I'm a class o'kids, it
might be easier to fucking talk then.

Joe I love him, but . . . he . . . he fucking kills me. (*Beat.*)
D'you know how it feels? To stand in a street in broad
daylight trying to sort your problems out? To stand outside a
pub on a Sunday afternoon and . . . you're talking to him
and you know he's off his face, and this big bastard comes up
– straight as a die, but he knows he can make his money
outa the queens – and he comes up and he says 'Here
Woody' and he hands him a little slip o'paper, the tiniest slip
o'paper with a little blue dot on it, and I feel that much of a
lowy I pay for it and the big bastard goes away. And then
your fella stands there and rips it in two, sticks one bit in his
pocket, and the other in his mouth . . . and keeps on talking
. . . About us, and the way we are, and the way . . . I make
him feel. 'You're hogging me Joe, I need me mates.' And I
just wanna say, 'Can't you wait five minutes? Can't you just
wait 'til I've gone and you're back with your mates? Can't
you take your acid then?' (*Shakes his head.*) I used to like me,
and the way I feel about me. But when you're with someone
else it's like . . . it's . . . well it's like you've got a mirror on
your shoulder, and what you see in them . . . is how you see
yourself. Like it's reflected. And if they're being a twat to you
. . . then . . . you think you're a twat yourself, you don't
question it. You can't. (*Beat.*) Am I talking shite?

Kenny Fucking shut up.

Kenny *lunges at* **Joe** *and snogs the face off him, rubbing his
shoulders as he does. He's really going for the kill. He pulls* **Joe**'s *top
up, pushes him onto the bed. As he does this he takes his own belt off.
On top of* **Joe**, *on the bed he pushes* **Joe**'s *arms above his head and
then ties his hands tightly to the top bed rail with the belt.*

Joe Jesus, what you doing?

Kenny I think it's time you enjoyed yourself!

Joe Untie me you bastard!

Kenny D'you want them kids to hear?

Joe What d'you think you're . . ?!

Kenny Let's get these jeans off.

Joe Oh my God! (*Laughs.*) I'm pissed as a fuckin' Newton and Ridley!

Kenny *has pulled* **Joe**'*s jeans down round his ankles. He has boxer shorts on.* **Kenny** *goes looking under the bed.*

Joe What you doing? Don't hurt me. Don't leave any marks!

Kenny *comes out from under the bed with a vibrator. He stands at the foot of the bed and waggles the vibrator in the air.*

Kenny Let's make babies!

Viv (*off*) Kenny! It's eleven o'clock! He's here!

Kenny Oh shit.

Viv (*off*) Kenny! He's in the bathroom getting changed!

Kenny (*to* **Joe**) Hang on, won't be a tick.

Joe Where you going?

Kenny Shut up!

Joe Lock the door!

Kenny Don't go away! (*Exits.*)

Joe *wriggles his wrists about. He can't release himself.*

Joe Oh mother forgive me! (*Laughs in desperation.*)

Elsewhere on the stage, lights up to reveal **Viv**'*s lounge.* **Simone**, **Kelly**, **Richard**, **Manda**, **Sonia** *and* **Viv** *are singing 'Happy Birthday' to* **Tammy**. *'Til the end of the scene, we can see the bedroom and the lounge at the same time.*

All Happy Birthday to you!
        Happy Birthday to you!

Happy Birthday dear Tammy!
Happy Birthday to you!

Whilst they sing this, **Kenny** *enters.*

Viv (*to* **Kenny**) He's in the bathroom! Get up and see if he's ready!

Kenny *exits. The singing finishes.*

Sonia Lovely.

Viv Not good enough. Do it again. Everybody this time, or you're all out!

They all sing 'Happy Birthday' again.

Viv (*to* **Manda**) Where's that tape? Give me that tape!

Manda *gets the tape from the first act out of her pocket and slips it to* **Viv**. *She sticks it in the music centre. The song finishes. Enter* **Kenny**.

Kenny Okay?

Viv Yep.

Kenny D'you want me to do an intro?

Viv Hurry up.

Kenny Now. Everyone got a drink?

David Where's Sir?

Kenny Bit tied up at the moment. Er, as you all know, this is Tammy's birthday party. And in an hour's time Tammy is going to be fourteen. Now it's been a hard year for Tammy, and Viv and Manda . . . what with Scottie dying and that. So we thought, tonight, to make it an extra special occasion, we'd invite an extra special guest.

Tammy East 17?!

Viv Shut up!

Kenny Now, she's come all the way from Buckingham Palace just to be here. So can we all be upstanding, for the one and only, Her Majesty, Queen Elizabeth the Second.

Viv switches the tape on. A trumpet fanfare plays. **Viv** *and* **Sonia** *hold* **Ivy** *up. A* **Drag Queen** *enters dressed as the Queen. He wears a long dress, sash, wig, crown, long white gloves and rings. He goes to the centre of the room and walks round in a circle, waving regally at the assembled company. When the trumpet fanfare ends, the National Anthem comes on and they all sing.* **Sonia** *and* **Viv** *curtsy when he turns to them, and they take* **Ivy** *down with them as they go. The kids are gobsmacked.*

Viv See who it is mum? It's the Queen.

David Tammy! Tammy! Is that a bloke?

Tammy It's the Queen!

David Why?

Tammy It's a laugh, init?

The National Anthem ends. The **Drag Queen** *speaks with a cockney twang.*

Queen Somebody get me a stiff gin.

Kenny Go on Manda.

Manda *tuts and exits.* **Richard** *goes to follow,* **Kenny** *pulls him back.*

Queen Who's the birthday girl?

Viv Tammy.

Tammy *steps forward.*

Queen Happy Birthday dear. You may kiss my ring. (*Holds his hand out to* **Tammy**. **Tammy** *kisses the ring on his finger.*) Have you sung Happy Birthday yet? (*Choruses of 'Yes'.*) Oh well sod that then. Oh hello Viv!

Viv All right Your Majesty?

Queen All these lovely boys and girls. (*To* **Simone**.) You gotta look of my Anne, dear.

Simone (*tuts*) Oh don't!

Queen Here, I had a bugger of a journey to get here.

Manda *comes in with two gins and gives one to the* **Queen**.

Queen Tar babe. Traffic was chock-a-block. We was stuck
in this traffic jam, me and my chauffeur, when this bloke in
the car next to me starts giving me the eye. I thought, funny.
Anyway, he keeps on winking. (**Viv** *laughs*.) I said winking,
you dirty bitch. The next thing I know is he's got his dick
out. Well I was outa that car like a flash. But d'you know
what? I was so excited, I fainted. Ooh what comes next? Oh
yeah. So I comes round and I'm lying there on the pavement
and there's this big copper standing over me.

Kenny Whoo!

Queen No Kenny, bigger than that. And he goes 'Your
Majesty, you must have had a stroke!' I goes, 'I should be so
lucky dear.' (*Laughter*.) Now stick the other side o'that tape
on Viv. I wanna get warbling. (*As* **Viv** *does this*.) Now can I
raise a toast to the birthday girl? What's your name again
love?

Tammy Tammy.

Queen To Tammy!

All To Tammy!

David *hasn't been enjoying this. He quietly makes his way out of the
room. The tape comes on. It is a backing track for 'I Am What I Am'.
The* **Queen** *sings. Everyone left in the room dances. Even* **Sonia** *is
boogieing on down.* **Ivy** *motions* **Kenny** *over, and he wheels her out
to go to the loo.* **Manda** *goes with them.*

Queen (*croony speaking as music warms up*) It takes a lifetime
         To become the best that we can be
         We have not the time or the right
         To judge each other
         It's one life and there's no return
         And no deposit
         One life
         So make sure you like what's in your closet.

         (*Sings*.) I am what I am
         I don't want praise, I don't want pity
         I bang my own drum
         Some think it's noise

I think it's pretty
And so what if I love each sparkle
And each bangle?
Why not try to see things from a different angle?
Your life is a sham
'Til you can shout out
I am what I am!
I am what I am!

(*Key change.*) I am what I am
And what I am needs no excuses
I deal my own deck
Sometimes the ace, sometimes the deuces
It's my life and I want to have a little pride in
My life
And it's not a place I have to hide in
Life's not worth a damn
'Til you can shout out
I am what I am!
I am what I am!

While all this is going on, **David** *appears in* **Viv**'s *bedroom.*

David Sir?

Joe David?

David Sir?

Joe Untie me, quick.

David Oh Jesus Sir!

Joe Hurry up!

David (*going to the belt*) Was it date rape Sir?

Joe Never mind that, just bloody untie me.

David I'll report her for you Sir.

Joe David . . .

David *unties the belt and* **Joe** *sits up. He hiccups.*

Joe You know you? You're all right you are. And d'you wanna know why?

David Put your clothes on Sir.

Joe Coz you're dead . . . you're dead . . . (*Can't think.*) David. Don't tell anyone.

David I won't.

Joe No you mustn't . . . coz it's all unspeakable.

David Sir you're me best teacher.

Joe Ah I know like but, you know . . .

David D'you wanna talk about it Sir?

Joe David? Phone me a taxi. I need to get a . . . a taxi, yeah?

David Right Sir. There's a cab office round the parade.

Joe We'll go downstairs, and we'll pretend it's for you. We'll make out I'm walking you to the taxi rank. Yeah?

David Nice one Sir.

Kenny *enters with a Tupperware bowl of whipped cream.*

Kenny (*coming in*) Joe? Got some whipped cream here Joe, and guess who's gonna be the . . . (*Sees* **David** *helping* **Joe** *up.*) dish.

David Thanks for a blinding party Mr Williams, but Sir's gonna walk me to a taxi rank init.

Kenny Joe!

David *leads* **Joe** *out.*

Joe (*to* **Kenny**) D'you know him? (*Points to* **David**.) He's bleedin' sound him! And d'you wanna know why?!

David Sir!

Joe (*to* **David** *as he leads him out*) You're dead cosmic you. You know that don't yeh?

They exit. **Kenny** *stands and stares. He dunks his finger in the bowl and takes a mouthful of cream.*

Manda *comes back into the lounge carrying an envelope.*

Manda Another letter mum.

Viv Let's see what the Lady of Letters has got to say for herself this time.

Kenny *comes out of the bedroom and heads downstairs.* **Viv** *rips the letter open and reads it.*

Sonia (*to* **Drag Queen**) Last time I danced like this was at a wedding in Caanan in Galilee. You know, you'd get on with my daughter. She loves experimenting with her appearance. Have you always had a wig?

Viv *switches the tape off.* **Richard** *is pawing at* **Manda**, *who looks at her mum.* **Kenny** *comes in without the bowl.*

Viv Oh shut up Sonia! (*Reads.*)

Simone (*to* **Tammy**) She was murdered once.

Tammy I know.

Simone By a woman with a blonde beehive and a handbag.

Sonia Shopping trolley! (*To* **Drag Queen**.) And d'you know who it was?

Viv I'll have her!

Manda What's it say mum?

Viv I'll fuckin' have her for this!

Sonia (*to* **Drag Queen**) Well it wasn't Valerie Pinkney!

Simone Can we have the music back on?

Viv Where is she?

Richard (*to* **Manda**) Anyone ever tell you you're fit?

Viv The evil cow.

Manda (*pushing* **Richard** *off*) Richard!

Viv Let me at her!

Tammy No mum!

Manda Knock her up mum!

Viv (*forcing back tears*) Says she's written to the council Sonia. Saying I neglect my kids. Do I neglect you Manda?

Manda You're never off me back.

Richard I'm jealous.

Viv The interfering lying little whore. I'll kill her!

Viv *makes for the door.* **Kenny** *grabs her, as do* **Tammy** *and* **Sonia**.

Tammy Mum!

Sonia Vivian think of the kids!

Kenny You stupid cow stay here!

Viv Off of me! I'll have her!

Sonia Calm down Vivian!

Manda *joins in and thumps their arms off her mother.* **Viv** *wrestles free. She runs from the room. Everyone tries to follow but* **Manda** *blocks the door, stopping them.*

End of scene. Straight into next.

Scene Five

Street

In the dark, lit only by streetlamps, **Viv** *appears, staggering into the street with the letter in her hand.*

Viv Written the council? You pissin' no mark! Working in a fuckin' launderette I'll have ya! Where are you? You can hear me, now get out here! Slappery little slap! I'm waiting! Pinkney get your flabby cheeks out here now!

Kenny *comes out of the house, followed by* **Manda**, **Tammy**, **Kelly**, **Richard**, *and then* **Sonia** *and the* **Drag Queen**.

Kenny Vivian!

Viv Keep away from me Kenny I'm warning you.

Kenny Come back in the house now! You'll only get hurt!

Viv She's hurting my girls!

Sonia It'll only end in tears Vivian.

Viv Good. Valerie!! Valerie!!

Manda Knock on her door mum!

Kenny Oi! Manda!

Manda Piss off!

Sonia Language!

Viv I'm waiting Valerie! Give you a taste of your own medicine! You fucking coward! (*To the others.*) She's gone too far this time.

Valerie Pinkney *steps outside, brush in hand. She's wearing a dressing gown, nightie and slippers. She stands with a hand on her hip.*

Val Say that again.

Viv I wouldn't waste my breath.

Val (*sniggers*) Look at you. Miss-Fanny-For-Lodgers, showing your knickers for all the street to see. Aint you got no pride? Wash it down the drain with the memory o'Scottie's name? Eh? Coming in at all hours. Different man every night.

Manda They're all queer!

Val Every time I open me curtains I got a bordello view and the stench o'Merry Widow. Women like you make me sick. Sick!

Viv How dare you spout all this bullshit about me.

Val Well it's a wise bull that knows its own shit.

Viv Come here and say that.

Valerie *walks over.*

Sonia Valerie don't.

Kenny Oi you touch her Pinkney . . .

Val It's a wise bull that knows its own shit.

Viv You little whore!

Viv *lunges at* **Val**. *They roll onto the floor fighting.* **Kenny** *runs over and tries to separate them.* **Manda** *runs over and tries to pull* **Kenny** *off. The* **Drag Queen** *and the* **Kids** *egg them on.*

Sonia Someone call the police!

David *leads* **Joe** *out of the house.*

Joe (*to* **Sonia**) What's going on girl? Oh it's all unspeakable.

Sonia Oh Mr Casey, phone the police! Phone the police!

Joe Aray girl I'm off me face. I'm bladdered.

David Taxi rank's this way Sir.

David *leads* **Joe** *off.*

Sonia *screams up to her house.*

Sonia Gemma! Gemma! Phone the police!

Tammy Don't Sonia!

Richard *decides to join in the fight, trying to save* **Manda**'s *skin.*

Sonia Gemma! Gemma!

A figure appears out of **Sonia**'s *front door.*

Sonia Gemma, how d'you get that door to open? Gemma?

Gemma *is dressed up in sixties clothes. Her blonde hair is up in a beehive and she pulls a shopping trolley. She speaks with a northern accent.*

Gemma Come little girl. Come with me!

Sonia *screams and collapses into the arms of the* **Drag Queen**. *A police siren wails in the distance, getting nearer all the time.*

The **Drag Queen** *lies* **Sonia** *on the floor and slaps her round the face trying to resuscitate her.*

Kelly Oright Gemma? You look good like that. Can hardly see your spots.

Viv *and* **Val** *still fighting.* **Kenny** *still trying to stop them.* **Simone** *lights a fag up and watches.* **Manda** *holds* **Richard** *off.* **Tammy** *starts to cry and screams down the street.* **Gemma** *takes* **Kelly**'*s fag off her and has a long drag, watching.*

Tammy Joe! Joe! Come back! Come and help me mum! Joe! Joe!

The police car gets nearer. Blackout.

In the blackout 'To Sir With Love' plays, by Lulu, linking to the next scene.

Scene Six

Joe'*s flat*

Lights up on **Joe** *sitting cock-eyed in the easy chair. He holds his stomach, groaning.*

Woody *comes in dressed for bed in boxies and a ravey long-sleeved sweatshirt, his hair skew-whiff. He holds an open bottle of Evian and a paracetamol tablet. He stands there.*

It's dark. A shaft of light creeps in from the kitchen.

Woody (*tenderly*) You soft get.

Joe I'll never live it down.

Woody What?

Joe Puking up in front of the kids like that.

Woody Well you will go gallivanting off to the backwaters of the Big Smoke. Come on. Take this. (*He squats down next to*

him.) It'll knock your hangover on the head in the morning.
(*Tries to give him the paracetamol.*)

Joe (*struggles with him*) I don't want that!

Woody It's a paracetamol!

Joe It's an E!

Woody It's a paracetamol!

Joe You're trying to kill me!

Pause. **Woody** *sighs.*

Woody God, you've got E on the brain.

Joe Is it any wonder living with you? Y'vile mong.

Woody Joey.

Joe What?

Woody You can always tell us to go you know.

Joe I know.

Woody It's your flat.

Joe I know. (*Beat.*) No it isn't. It's our flat.

Woody If I'm doing your head in.

Joe Shut up will yer?

Woody You told us to before.

Joe Where did you go?

Woody Stormed off down the street. Went and sat in the
launderette, watching other people's crusty undies going
round. Got back just in time for the feature length edition of
Taggart. So I numbed me brain on half o'pound o'telly. Was
the party shite?

Joe Yeah.

Woody Acting straight. Avoiding all references to Doris Day.

Joe I know, it really takes it out of yer.

Pause.

So you never went the Fridge?

Woody No.

Joe And you never done E?

Woody No.

Joe I wish you'd done E.

Woody (*tenderly*) You dickhead.

Joe I know. That's why you love me.

Woody I know yeah.

Woody *gets on the chair with him and puts his arm round him. He chuckles quietly and then kisses* **Joe** *softly on the head.*

Scene Seven

School playground

The next Monday back at school. A tall wire mesh fence separates the playground from the playing fields. **David** *sits huddled in a corner to the left, the other side of the fence, hugging a football.*

Kelly, **Simone** *and* **Richard** *are walking away from him, this side of the fence, sharing a cigarette inconspicuously. When taking a drag they turn their back to the school (audience).*

When they've just about reached the right end of the fence, **Joe Casey** *enters with his school bag. He stops to talk to* **David**. *The others hastily stub out their fag and walk briskly to the front of the stage and off.*

Joe Morning, David.

David Sir.

From the way **David** *speaks it is obvious he is crying.*

Joe David? What's the matter?

David Nothing. Leave me alone.

David *jumps up and runs right, quickly, along the side of the fence.*

Joe David!

David *stops and, holding onto the fence, stares through at* **Joe**. *Then he runs again, round the fence and in the direction of the school.* **Joe** *raises his voice.*

Joe David Dobson stop right there!!

Joe's *tone is severe.* **David** *freezes.* **Joe** *walks towards him.*

Joe What's been said David?

David I can't say, it's not nice.

Joe (*more insistent*) David?

David I wish I'd never gone to that fucking party!

Joe There's no need to swear David.

David Oh . . . (*Wants to swear but can't bring himself to.*)

Joe Oh fucking swear then.

David It's Kelly, and Simone. They reckon they're gonna spread it round the whole class that I wanted to have sex with Tammy. And I never, I swear. All we talked about was . . . in moderation.

Joe *starts to chuckle.*

David And Richard reckons he's gonna tell everyone you dance like a queer.

Joe (*chuckles*) Is that all?

David Oh that's easy for you to say.

Joe True. (*Puts his arm round* **David**.) This sex. It's a scarey business isn't it?

David You're telling me.

Joe I'll have words with them.

David Don't tell 'em I said nothing.

Joe Don't worry. I owe you one.

David Cheers Sir. I can call you Sir now, what a relief. Sir?

Joe What?

David What happened the other night. What Tammy's uncle done to you. It aint right, is it?

Joe Well. Takes all sorts to make a world.

David Right.

Joe Have a hanky. (*Gets a tissue out of his bag for him.*)

David Tar.

Joe Now come on, or we'll both be late.

Joe and **David** *walk towards the school.*

David Tammy aint gonna be in today Sir.

Joe Surprise surprise.

David I knocked for her and her mum said they've all got twenty-four-hour flu. Yeah well, we all know what that means, don't we eh?

They keep walking.

Did you puke in the taxi Sir?

Joe No.

David Oh that's good.

Joe Aye.

David Coz it's a fiver extra if you do Sir.

They exit. Seven warning pips herald the start of a new school day.

Lightning Source UK Ltd.
Milton Keynes UK
25 February 2011

168246UK00001B/33/P